MAKING CONNECTIONS 1:
An Integrated Approach to Learning English
TEACHER'S EXTENDED EDITION

Carolyn Kessler

Linda Lee

Mary Lou McCloskey

Mary Ellen Quinn

Lydia Stack

Contributing Writer

Carolyn Bohlman

Heinle & Heinle Publishers
An International Thomson Publishing Company
Boston, MA 02116, U.S.A.

I(T)P

The publication of *Making Connections* was directed by the members of the Heinle & Heinle Secondary ESL Publishing Team:

Editorial Director:	Roseanne Mendoza
Senior Production Services Coordinator:	Lisa McLaughlin
Market Development Director:	Ingrid Greenberg
Developmental Editor:	Nancy Jordan

Also Participating in the publication of this program were:

Publisher:	Stan Galek
Director of Production:	Elizabeth Holthaus
Manufacturing Coordinator:	Mary Beth Hennebury
Composition:	Prepress Company, Inc.
Project Management:	Carole Rollins
Interior Design:	Carole Rollins/Martucci Studio
Illustration:	Jerry Malone/Martucci Studio
Cover Design:	Martucci Studio

Manufactured in the United States of America

ISBN: 0-8384-7001-7

Heinle & Heinle Publishers is an International Thomson Publishing Company

10   9   8   7   6   5   4   3   2   1

▲▲▲

Contents

Unit 1 - Getting Around School

Topics

Unit 2 - Spending Free Time

Topics

Unit 3 - Counting Dollars and Cents

Topics

Unit 4 - Choosing Clothes

Topics

Unit 5 - Checking the Weather

Topics

Unit 6 - Making Journeys

Topics

Unit 7 - Solving Problems

Topics

Unit 8 - Exploring Diversity

Topics

TO THE TEACHER

Goals, Philosophy

Middle and High School ESOL (English for Speakers of Other Languages) students are faced with a formidable task. In the few short years of school that remain, they must learn both English and the challenging content of their academic curriculum, made more challenging because so much language acquisition is demanded. *Making Connections: An Integrated Approach to Learning English* provides resources to integrate the teaching and learning of language and academic content. Resources in the series help teachers and students develop students' ability to communicate in English as they focus on motivating themes with topics, activities, tools, and procedures that introduce the content areas of science, social studies, and literature.

We are aware of the need for materials that help us to teach to the long-term learning goals we know are most important, and to teach the ways we know students learn best. We know this from our own experiences as teachers, as well as from working and talking with many classroom teachers. *Making Connections: An Integrated Approach to Learning English* is designed to do both: to help secondary students and their teachers reach toward important, essential goals, and to facilitate their learning language and content in the ways they learn best. What are the goals we reach for?

Joy—the joy in life and learning that will make our students happy, successful life-time learners;

Literacy—the ability to use reading and writing to accomplish amazing things;

Community—the knowledge that they live in an accepting community where they have rights, responsibilities, and resources;

Access—access to whatever resources they need to accomplish their own goals—including access to technology;

Power—the power to make their lives into whatever they choose.

What are the ways of teaching and learning that work best, according to our best understanding of language acquisition research? The answer, we believe, is **integrated learning**. In *Making Connections,* we include four different kinds of integration: integration of language areas, of language and academic content, of students with one another, and of school with the larger community.

- **We integrate language areas through active learning.**

We combine reading, writing, listening, and speaking into things that students do. Through interacting with authentic and culturally relevant literature, through activities that involve genuine communication, and through student-owned process writing, students learn the "parts" or "skills" of language in meaningful "whole" contexts.

- **We integrate language with academic content and process.**

Language is best learned when it is used as a tool; when students are meaningfully engaged in something important to them. Learning the language of and participating in processes specific to academic content area subjects are essential for preparing students to move into mainstream content-area classrooms. By teaching language through content, we attempt to do several things at once: we help students to learn to use a variety of learning strategies, we introduce them to science, social studies, and literature content appropriate for their age and grade level, and we help them use accessible language and learn new and essential language in the process.

- **We integrate students with one another.**

We try to help teachers and students develop a real learning community, in which students and teachers use a variety of strategies—including many cooperative learning strategies—to accomplish student-owned educational goals. We acknowledge that students are not all at the same level linguistically or academically, but we recognize that each student has strengths to offer in your classroom, so we provide choices of materials and activities that accomodate a multi-level class.

- **We integrate school with home culture and with the greater community.**

We strive for materials and activities that are relevant for a culturally diverse group and that help students to develop their self-esteem by valuing their unique cultural heritages. We seek to involve students in the community, and the community in students, by providing and encouraging activities and projects that relate to community life and that put students into interaction with community representatives. This active involvement is integral to the development of students' content-area knowledge and language.

In order to reach toward these goals and implement these four kinds of integration, we have used integrated thematic units as the organizational basis for *Making Connections*. Other themes are arrived at in a variety of ways. Some, such as "Checking the Weather," have very concrete connections among the sections of the units. Others,

such as "Sending Messages," make more metaphorical connections among sections that treat very different aspects of themes. In all the units, students will make connections across content areas and will revisit themes and use and re-use the language of a theme in different ways. Each unit provides multi-level information and experiences that integrate language and one or more content areas, and includes the following features:

Learning Strategies

In each unit, we highlight strategies to help students with their language and content area learning. We encourage teachers and students to be aware of the applicability of these strategies in new learning situations. Our goal is to create active, capable, self-starting learners. Research has shown that students apply learning strategies while learning a second language. These strategies have been classified, and they include:

> **Metacognitive Strategies,** through which students think about their own learning processes.
>
> **Cognitive Strategies,** which relate directly to learning tasks and often involve direct manipulation or transformation of learning materials.
>
> **Social/Affective Strategies,** which involve teacher and peer interaction to accomplish learning goals.

Many of these strategies can be used as **Mediation Strategies,** strategies through which learning is assisted. Transfer of learning strategies from one context to another can be enhanced by combining cognitive and metacognitive strategies. In developing *Making Connections* we have constantly sought ways to assist students in developing their own repertoire of learning strategies. Following are strategies included in the series.

1. Reading Strategies: We encourage you to use a variety of ways to guide students through the reading selections. To accomodate the varied levels of students, you might choose one or a combination of these strategies for reading the selections:

A. *Read Aloud:* You or an advanced student read the selection aloud to the students. Pay attention to your voice. Develop your expressiveness, varying pitch, volume, and speed of reading. Create different voices for different characters when reading literature selections. Don't read too quickly since second language learners need time to process what is read.

B. *Shared Reading:* Teacher and students read together using text on a transparency or a chart or multiple copies of the selection. During shared reading, students at a variety of language levels can all participate in different ways.

C. *Paired Reading:* Two students take turns reading aloud to each other. If they are reading prose, one student can read one paragraph, and the next student can read the following paragraph. If they are reading poetry, students can alternate lines or stanzas.

D. *Silent Reading:* Provide time during class for your students to read. Students need plenty of reading material at different reading levels, selections from text as well as other sources. Set clear expectations for your students during the silent reading time. Everyone must read; they cannot talk or write during this time.

E. *Directed Reading:* Students learning to read in English often need help with their acquisition since content-area schemata may be culturally specific and not part of the second language learner's cultural background. To make difficult material accessible, the teacher divides text into manageable "chunks" and uses strategies such as questions, outlines, or story maps to support student reading. The following activities help students acquire schema:

1. *Use questions as a "scaffolding" technique.* The use of questions helps to clarify meanings of words, develop concepts, encourage both literal and inferential comprehension, and relate the story to the students' own experiences. For multilevel classes, include questions at a variety of levels, from labeling and recall to analysis. Always include some questions that do not have just one right answer, in order to encourage students to think for themselves.

2. *Use cueing strategies.* When reading literature selections with various characters, use verbal cueing strategies, such as changes of voice for different characters, pauses to indicate changes in events and dramatic moments, and exaggerated intonation for key words and concepts. Use non-verbal cueing strategies, such as pointing to illustrations or parts of illustrations, and using facial expressions, gestures, and actions to accompany key events in the story. Story maps or content-area charts can also serve as cues. (See graphic organizers)

F. *Independent Reading:* Encourage students to read outside of class. Take students to the school or public library, and encourage them to use this resource often. Help them select reading materials at their interest and reading levels. If possible, develop a classroom library and provide class time for independent silent reading of self-selected materials. Read yourself during this time to serve as a role model.

2. Graphic Organizers: Graphic organizers are visual aids that help students remember the content as they read and then relate that content to their own experience. Graphic organizers can be used in many stages of unit study. As pre-reading activities they prepare students for the text they will read. During a reading, graphic organizers help students understand what they are reading, and after the reading, graphic organizers help students analyze what they have read. Finally, graphic organizers can be used as pre-writing activities, to help students organize material for writing stories, essays, and reports. Many graphic organizers are used in *Making Connections*. Some of these are described below.

A. *Semantic Maps:* Semantic mapping includes a variety of ways to make graphic displays of information within categories related to a central concept. This strategy helps students to demonstrate prior knowledge and add new information. The semantic maps can show relationships among terms and concepts and help students to develop vocabulary, improve understanding, review material learned, and prepare to write.

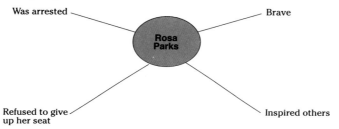

A Semantic Map

B. *Five Point Outline:* This graphic organizer helps students to generate basic information to prepare for writing by asking the basic newswriter questions. The students draw rays coming from a "sun" center and write a question word on each ray: Who, What, When, Where, Why. Then students write a phrase or two about the writing topic that answers each question.

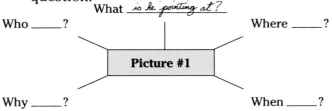

A Five Point Outline

C. *Venn Diagram:* A Venn Diagram uses circles to show similarities and differences between topics or concepts. Two overlapping circles allow students to compare and contrast information. Information that is common to both topics or concepts is written in the overlapping part of the circles. Information that is specific to one or the other of the topics or concepts is written in the circle for that topic or concept.

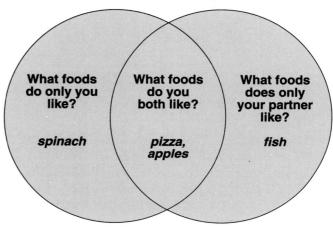

A Venn Diagram

D. *K/W/L Chart:* The Know/Want to Know/Learned (K/W/L) Chart is a preparatory activity that allows students to discover what they know about a given topic and what they want to know. Before beginning to study a topic,

Know	Want to know	Learned
What do you know about the story from the pictures?	What do you want to know?	What did you learn?
Younde lives in a village.	*Where is the village?*	

A K/W/L Chart

students make a chart with two columns. At the top of one column, they write "Know" and at the top of the other column they write "Want to Know." Students meet in small groups and talk about the topic. They also brainstorm questions they want answered about the topic. In the first column students write things they know about the subject, and in the second column they write questions they want answered about the topic. After studying a topic, you may want to add a third column to the chart "Learned," and have students work in groups or with you to write information they have learned while studying this topic.

E. *Graphs:* Graphs are visual displays of data or information that help students' understanding of the information presented. A graph allows students to compare data or information.

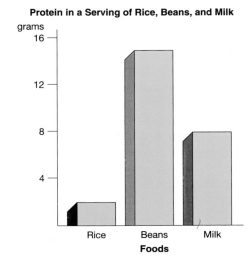

Protein in a Serving of Rice, Beans, and Milk

A Graph

A Timeline

F. *Timelines:* Timelines allow students to organize information chronologically, and often to gain an historical perspective. If events happen over time, a timeline can help students match dates to events.

3. Cooperative Learning: Cooperative learning has been shown to be effective in facilitating both student learning and successful cross-cultural, multi-level student integration. Each unit uses a variety of cooperative groups and activities to achieve these goals. Some of the cooperative learning techniques used in *Making Connections* are:

A. *Jigsaw:* Divide up a task as if it were a jigsaw puz zle. The members of the home group can each become an expert in a small part of the task. Then, when they fit the pieces together, everyone understands the whole. For a reading selection:
1. Divide the reading selection into one part for each group member (4–6 students per group).
2. Each person becomes an expert on one part. To become an expert, students study the reading selection closely.
3. Then each person retells his or her part of the reading selection to the group and the home group can ask questions of the expert.
4. Either groups or individuals then answer questions on the entire reading.

B. *Think–Pair–Share:*
1. Students think about an experience they have had that is related to the topic they are studying.
2. In pairs, students tell their experience to each other. Students take notes as they listen to their partners to prepare to retell their partners' experiences.
3. Two pairs of students get together and each student tells his/her partner's experience to the group.

C. *Choral Reading:* Two or more students read a poem, a story, or a play out loud in unison.

Divide the selection and students into high voice parts, medium voice parts, and low voice parts. Students practice reading in their groups until they can read their parts in unison; then the three groups come together to read their parts of the selection in the correct order.

Language Focus

Language is learned best in meaningful, useful contexts. From meaningful contexts, many opportunities arise to teach language concepts as they are needed. In *Making Connections,* we have provided suggestions both in the student texts and in the teacher editions for teaching language features as opportunities arise in the text materials or in the language students are using.

Although learners of English are not yet proficient in using English, they are proficient users of another language or languages, have had many academic and non-academic experiences, and are capable of high-level thinking. Language educators are challenged to provide appropriate materials for these students, materials that challenge them intellectually without frustrating them linguistically. The carefully-chosen reading selections in *Making Connections* provide students models of high-quality language, with the sophistication and complexity appropriate to the students' age levels. Readings offer new vocabulary in context and serve as a source for learning about the mechanics of language in authentic contexts. Reading selections provide a common text that students can use to negotiate meaning and to participate in lively discussions about the topics.

Each unit of *Making Connections* includes a number of Language Focus boxes that use content and context as opportunities to suggest practice in using particular language forms and functions. We encourage you to use these Language Focus boxes to inspire contextualized practice—drills, conversations, dialogues, and chants, for example—to build your students' language abilities.

Content-area experiences in science, social studies, and literature

We have chosen three content areas for focus in *Making Connections* because of their importance to student success and because of the importance of language to success in these areas. In science, we introduce the language of science (and frequently mathematics language as well) through offering authentic scientific experiences with materials that are accessible to an ESOL teacher. In social studies, we take advantage of the multicultural nature of ESOL classes to introduce the processes of the social sciences—the study of history, geography, culture, and economics. In the content area of literature, we have provided a variety of genres to enhance content-area learning as students begin to learn the language they need to talk about literary works and move on to create their own.

Writing

Making Connections applies a process approach to writing: it offers students opportunities to select topics and experiment with writing activities using themes and forms inspired by the science, social science, and literature content. We have included activities at all stages of the writing process including Prewriting, Drafting, Responding to One Another's Writing, Revising, Editing, and Publishing. We want students to see the writing process as something they can do and we want them to see authors as real people.

Choices for Teachers and Students

Every ESOL class is a multi-level, multicultural class. In order to meet the needs of these diverse groups, and in order to empower both teachers and students, *Making Connections* offers many choices. Teachers can choose among the many activities in the units to provide experiences most appropriate to their classes and can sequence these activities as needed. They can also individualize by choosing different activities for different students in the class. Each unit includes an Activity Menu of experiences and projects that will help students to integrate and apply the material from the unit. Both teacher and students can make choices among these culminating events to suit them to student interest, level of ability, and needs.

COMPONENTS OF THE MAKING CONNECTIONS PROGRAM

Student text

Making Connections: An Integrated Approach to Learning English integrates the teaching and learning of language and academic content. The student text provides students opportunities to develop their ability to communicate in English as they focus on motivating themes with topics, activities, tools, and procedures that introduce the content areas of science, social studies, and literature.

The Activity Menu at the end of each unit provides opportunities to help students relate their learnings around the unit theme to one another and to review and explore further concepts developed in the unit. Following each unit is a collection of supplemental readings related to the unit topics. We have included these readings in response to requests from pilot teachers for more literary selections related to unit topics.

Teacher's Extended Edition

This Teacher's Extended Edition provides:
- an introduction to the thematic, integrated teaching approach
- a description of several approaches to presenting literature selections
- a guide to the study strategies that appear in the student book
- detailed teaching suggestions for each activity
- suggestions for extension activities
- listening scripts

Workbooks

Workbooks provide additional practice in using the vocabulary, language functions, language structures, and study strategies introduced in each of the thematic units. Workbook activities can be used in class or assigned as homework.

CD-ROM

This lively, fun, user-friendly program features highly interactive units that parallel the student text. Students engage in sentence completion, interact with videos, create notes from a variety of sources, and complete graphs and charts. Also included is a writing area, an additional language practice section, and printing scorecards for each unit. The program is colorful, easy to navigate and offers a help feature on every screen.

Literacy Masters

Literacy Masters provide special support for pre-literate students. These materials are designed for students who enter the program at the Preproduction or Early Production stage. (Students who have only minimal comprehension of English.) The materials correspond with the units of Making Connections I and are very useful in multilevel classes.

The Teacher's Guide to the Heinle & Heinle ESL Program

The Heinle & Heinle ESL Program consists of the two series: *Making Connections 1, 2, and 3*, and *Voices in literature, Bronze, Silver, and Gold*, which can be used independently or together. The Teacher's Guide th the Heinle & Heinle ESL Program provides much practical advice and strategies for using the two series together. In this guide, classroom practitioners will learn how to take advantage of the revisitation of terms, themes, content and literature are organized thematically, students can continuously relate and analyze academic concepts and literary works. This Teacher's Guide also offers strategies fro providing instruction to students at many levels—from beginning English language proficiency to advanced levels of content-based and literature-based instruction. A technology section describes how instructors can use electronic support, such as e-mail and software, to expand on the activities found in *Making Connections* and *Voices in Literature*.

Assessment Program

The Assessment Program consists of several components and accommodates a range of assessment philosophies and formats. Included are:

- a portfolio assessment kit, complete with a teacher's guide to using portfolios and forms for student and teacher evaluation
- two "progress checks" per unit
- one comprehensive test per unit

Transparencies

Color Transparencies provide enlargements of visuals from the student texts. Many teachers find it helpful to view visuals with the students as they point out details. They may also write on pages using blank overlay transparencies.

Activity Masters

Reproducible activity masters support activities from the student book by providing write-on forms and graphic organizers for student's use. Activities for use with these masters consistently promote active student roles in engaging experiences.

Tape Program

Audio Tapes provide opportunities for group and individual extended practice with the series materials. The tapes contain all the listening activities included in the student texts. Scripts of the recorded material are included in the Teacher's Extended Edition.

ABOUT THE AUTHORS

Carolyn Kessler

Carolyn Kessler is Professor of English as a Second Language/Applied Linguistics at the University of Texas at San Antonio where she teaches graduate courses for the master's degree in ESL. She serves extensively as a consultant to school districts for ESL programs and has published widely on bilingualism, second language learning, and literacy. She has taught ESL both in the United States and abroad and is a former secondary language and science teacher.

Linda Lee

Linda Lee is an ESL/EFL teacher and writer. She has taught in the United States, Italy, China, and Iran.

Mary Lou McCloskey

Mary Lou McCloskey coordinates the Atlanta Satellite of the University of Oklahoma Bilingual Education Center. She has developed integrated curriculum and consulted with school districts across the United States. She is past second vice president of International TESOL.

Mary Ellen Quinn

Mary Ellen Quinn is Visiting Professor of Mathematics at Our Lady of the Lake University. As a consultant in science and ESL to school districts throughout the country, she has presented many papers on bilingualism and science education both nationally and internationally and has published in those areas. She has been curriculum director for elementary and secondary schools as well as a secondary school teacher of ESL, science and mathematics.

Lydia Stack

Lydia Stack is resource teacher for the Mentor Teacher and New Teacher programs for San Francisco Unified School District. She was formerly the ESL Department Head at Newcomer High School in San Francisco, and has consulted widely with school districts across the United States in the areas of curriculum development and teacher training. She is past president of International TESOL.

MAKING CONNECTIONS 1:

An Integrated Approach to Learning English

Carolyn Kessler

Linda Lee

Mary Lou McCloskey

Mary Ellen Quinn

Lydia Stack

Heinle & Heinle Publishers
A Division of Wadsworth, Inc.
Boston, MA 02116, U.S.A.

MAKING CONNECTIONS *Book 1*

FUNCTIONS	STRUCTURES	STUDY STRATEGIES
Introducing Yourself and Other People Telling Where People Are From Telling the Time Locating Places Asking and Answering Questions About Class Schedules Expressing Likes and Dislikes	Present Tense: *be, like* "Wh" Questions: *where, what* Yes/No Questions: Present Tense Subject Pronouns Possessive Adjectives	Selective Listening Reading a Class Schedule Making a Chart
Expressing Likes and Dislikes Comparing Likes and Dislikes Making and Responding to Suggestions Describing Daily Routines	Present Tense: Affirmative Present Tense: Negative Yes/No Questions: Affirmative and Negative *Let's . . .* (formulaic) *I'd love to . . .* (formulaic)	Classifying Making a Venn Diagram Evaluating Making a Cluster Diagram Reading a Chart
Identifying Amounts of Money Asking and Answering Questions About Prices Guessing Comparing Prices Ordering Food	"Wh" Questions: *who, which, how much* Present Tense Comparative Forms of Adjectives *I'd like . . .* (formulaic) *That'll be . . .* (formulaic)	Making a Chart Selective Listening Selective Reading
Identifying Clothes Describing Clothes Expressing Likes and Dislikes Comparing Clothes Giving Reasons Making Plans	"Wh" Questions: *what, which, why* Present Tense Present Continuous Object Pronouns Comparative Forms of Adjectives *Because* Future with *be going to*	Selective Listening Making a Chart Interviewing Quickwriting Writing a Poem

MAKING CONNECTIONS *Book 1*

LANGUAGE FOCUS: FUNCTIONS	LANGUAGE FOCUS: STRUCTURES	STUDY STRATEGIES
Identifying Weather Conditions Predicting the Weather Describing Weather Conditions Comparing Temperatures Guessing	Present Continuous Future with *be going to* Simple Past Comparative Form of Adjectives Superlative Form of Adjectives	Reading a Map Reading a Line Graph Making a Story Map Selective Listening
Locating Countries Identifying Possible Ways to Travel Evaluating Forms of Transportation Describing Places Giving Reasons Locating Places in North America Planning a Trip	Present Tense *can/can't* Questions with *can* Superlative Form of Adjectives Adverbs of Manner "Wh" Questions: *what, where, when, why, how* Future with *will*	Reading a Map Classifying Making a Chart Using Pictures Analyzing Using a Formula Making a Cluster Diagram
Identifying Problems and Solutions Making Predictions (Guessing) Describing a Sequence of Events in the Past Guessing Suggesting Possible Solutions Giving Instructions	Simple Past *Could/Couldn't* "Wh" Questions: *who, what, where, why, how* Commands	Using Pictures Selective Reading Making a Plot Profile
Identifying Similarities and Differences Giving Information About Yourself and Others Describing a Sequence of Events in the Past	Present Tense Simple Past *and, but* "Wh" Questions: *who, what, where, when, why*	Making a Venn Diagram Reading a Chart Making a Story Map Selective Reading Using Context Taking Notes in a Chart Interviewing Making a Cluster Diagram

ACKNOWLEDGMENTS

The authors want to thank colleagues, students, and teachers from whom we have learned much and who have offered strong and encouraging support for this project. We thank Chris Foley, Roseanne Mendoza, Nancy Mann, Elaine Leary, and Lisa McLaughlin for their support in the development and production of this project and for weathering with us the storms and challenges of doing something so new. Our expert office staff—Josie Cressman and Sherrie Tindle—provided intelligent and efficient assistance always accompanied by friendship, and we are appreciative. We also want to thank family members—Erin, Dierdre, and Jim Stack; Kevin and Sean O'Brien, and Joel and Tom Reed—for their love and support during this project.

The publisher and authors wish to thank the following teachers who pilot tested the *Making Connections* program. Their valuable feedback on teaching with these materials greatly improved the final product. We are grateful to all of them for their dedication and commitment to teaching with the program in a prepublication format.

Elias S. Andrade and Gudrun Draper
James Monroe High School
North Hills, CA

Nadine Bagel
Benjamin Franklin Middle School
San Francisco, CA

Kate Bamberg
Newcomer High School
San Francisco, CA

Kate Charles
Sycamore Junior High School
Anaheim, CA

Anne Elmkies, Irene Killian, and Kay Stark
Hartford Public Schools
Hartford, CT

Genoveva Goss
Alhambra High School
Alhambra, CA

Margaret Hartman
Lewisville High School
Lewisville, TX

Carmen N. Jimenez
Intermediate School 184
New York, NY

Rob Lamont and Judith D. Clark
Trimble Technical High School
Fort Worth, TX

Judi Levin
Northridge Middle School
Northridge, CA

Ligita Longo
Spring Woods High School
Houston, TX

Mary Makena
Rancho Alamitas High School
Garden Grove, CA

Alexandra M. McHugh
Granby, CT

Beatrice W. Miranda
Leal Middle School
San Antonio, TX

Doris Partan
Longfellow School
Cambridge, MA

Jane Pierce
Douglas MacArthur High School
San Antonio, TX

Cynthia Prindle
Thomas Jefferson High School
San Antonio, TX

Sydney Rodrigues
Doig Intermediate School
Garden Grove, CA

Cecelia Ryan
Monte Vista High School
Spring Valley, CA

Patsy Thompson
Gwinnett Vocational Center
Lawrenceville, GA

Fran Venezia
North Dallas High School
Dallas, TX

The publisher and authors would also like
to thank the following people who reviewed
the *Making Connections* program at various
stages of development. Their insights and
suggestions are much appreciated.

Suzanne Barton
Fort Worth Independent School District
Forth Worth, TX

Keith Buchanan
Fairfax County Public Schools
Fairfax, VA

Carlos Byfield
San Diego City College
San Diego, CA

John Croes
Lowell High School
Lowell, MA

Flo Decker
El Paso, TX

Lynn Dehart
North Dallas High School
Dallas, TX

Cecilia Esquer
El Monte High School
El Monte, CA

Marge Gianelli
Canutillo Independent School District
El Paso, TX

Nora Harris
Harlandale Independent School District
San Antonio, TX

Richard Hurst
Holbrook High School
Holbrook, AZ

Betty J. Mace-Matluck
Southwest Educational Development
  Laboratory
Austin, TX

Jacqueline Moase-Burke
Oakland Independent School District
Oakland, MI

Jeanne Perrin
Boston Public Schools
Boston, MA

Ron Reese
Long Beach Unified School District
Long Beach, CA

Linda Sasser
Alhambra School District
Alhambra, CA

Donna Sievers
Garden Grove Unified School District
Garden Grove, CA

Stephen F. Sloan
James Monroe High School
North Hills, CA

Dorothy Taylor
Adult Learning Center
Buffalo Public Schools
Buffalo, NY

Beth Winningham
James Monroe High School
North Hills, CA

Making Connections 1:
An Integrated Approach to Learning English
TEACHER'S EXTENDED EDITION

Language Focus

- This is Fernando. He is from Mexico.
- This is Marta. She is from Russia.

Claudia ◄

Satoshi ►

Ali ▲

Getting Around School

◄ Nadine

◄ Fernando

▼ Marta

1. Listen

a. Classwork. Listen and find the person.

Student text page 1

Activity 1: Listen

1. *Part a.* Introduce this activity by reading aloud the sentences in the Language Focus box. Have students point to the pictures of Fernando and Marta. Ask more proficient students about the people in the pictures. For example, *How many girls are there? How many boys are there? Where do you think Satoshi is from?*

2. Read the script or play the tape. Have students listen and point to the person being introduced. Then point to each student in the picture and say: *This is Satoshi. He is from* _____ . Let students complete the sentences.

(Continued on page 2.)

Activity 1: Listen *(continued)*

3. *Parts b and c.* Give each student a copy of Activity Master 1/1 (AM 1/1) or have them copy the chart on page 2. Read aloud the information about Fernando in the first Language Focus box. Use a checkmark to record this information in the chart on AM 1/1, and encourage students to do the same. Let a volunteer tell about Marta, and have students add this information to their chart. Warn them not to write any answers in the book.

4. Let students work on their own or in pairs to complete their charts.

5. Have students take turns telling about the people in the chart, using the model in the Language Focus box.

Activity 2: Introduce Yourself

1. *Part a.* Model the activity by introducing yourself to a student, using the model in the second Language Focus box. Then let two students introduce themselves, using the sample dialogue. Call attention to the last line in the Language Focus box, *I'm = I am.* Point out that *I'm* is a short way of saying *I am.* Next, put students in pairs to introduce themselves.

2. *Part b.* Read aloud the sentences in the Language Focus box on page 3 while students look at the picture on page 1. Then have volunteers introduce the other students in the picture. For example, *This is Satoshi. He's from Japan.* Call attention to the last two lines in the Language Focus box, and explain the use of *He's* and *She's.*

3. As a follow-up activity, play a memory game. Ask students to sit in a circle. Begin the game by introducing yourself. For example, *I'm Mr. Gonzalez. I'm from Canada.* The student next to you says, *This is Mr. Gonzalez. He's from Canada. I'm Anna. I'm from Poland.* The next student introduces both you and the first student and then tells about her/himself. The last student must introduce everyone in the circle and then tell about him/herself.

4. For additional practice, have students make a chart with information about the class, using the model at the top of page 2.

b. On your own. Where are these students from? Mark your answer in a chart like this.

Where are they from?						
	Colombia	**Japan**	**Haiti**	**Iran**	**Mexico**	**Russia**
Fernando					✓	
Marta						
Satoshi						
Nadine						
Ali						
Claudia						

Language Focus

- Fernando is from Mexico.
- Marta is from
  _____ .

Language Focus

A: Hi. My name is Fernando. I'm from Mexico.
B: Hi. I'm Marta. I'm from Russia.
I'm = I am

c. Compare answers with your classmates.

_____ is from _____ .

2. Introduce Yourself

a. Pairwork. Introduce yourself to a partner.

A: Hi. My name is _____

I'm from _____

B: Hi. I'm _____

I'm from _____

b. Introduce your partner to the class.

This is ——————— . He's from ——————— .

This is ——————— . She's from ——————— .

3. **Play a Game**

a. Classwork. Write your first name on a card like this:

> *Maria*

Give your card to your teacher.

b. On your own. Introduce yourself to nine classmates. Write their names in a chart like this.

Maria	Lan	Alisha
Anh	Rocco	Fernando
Ben	Nicole	Ahmad

c. Follow your teacher's instructions to play a game of bingo.

Language Focus

■ This is Fernando. He's from Mexico.

■ This is Marta. She's from Russia.

He's = He is
She's = She is

Activity 3: Play a Game

1. *Part a.* Give each student a blank card and have them print their name on it. Collect the cards and put them in a bag. You can complete a card and play the game too.

2. *Part b.* Give each student a copy of AM 1/2 or have them draw a grid with nine squares. Model this part of the activity by introducing yourself to several students in the class, using the sample dialogue on page 2. Write these students' names in random order in the boxes on AM 1/2. Ask a volunteer to introduce herself to several students and then to add their names to her activity master. Students should notice that the charts will be different.

3. Ask students to stand up and move around the classroom while they introduce themselves to nine students in the class. They should then write the names of these classmates in their chart. Circulate to support less proficient students.

4. *Part c.* Play the game the first time to clarify the rules. Have one student draw a card from the bag and read the name to the class. Ask the named person to raise a hand (to help students learn each other's names). Have students look for this student's name on their chart. If they find it, they should place a paper clip or other small object in that square. Repeat with other cards in the bag. The first person to get a row of names horizontally, vertically or diagonally says "Bingo" and wins the game. Put the name cards in the bag and play the game again. Small prizes like a new pencil or a bookmark can be provided.

Activity 4: Analyze

1. *Part a.* Introduce the activity by drawing a clock on the board with the time set at 4 o'clock. Ask: *What time is it?* Change the hands to show the following times: 4:10, 4:15, 4:30, 4:45, and 4:55, each time repeating the question and eliciting answers. Have students look at the nine clocks in the book. Point to each clock and ask: *What time is it?* Students can respond chorally.

2. With less proficient students, provide additional practice by using a clock with moveable hands. Let student 1 set the hands and then ask student 2 the time. Student 2 answers and then sets a different time for student 3, and so on.

3. Point to each picture on pages 4 and 5 and ask: *Where is Tran?* Go in order of pictures, not in time order. Let more proficient students tell what the people are doing in each picture.

4. Read aloud the question in the Language Focus box. Let students find the picture and answer your question. Then ask: *Where is Tran at eleven forty-five?* Again let students find the picture and answer the question.

5. Give pairs of students a copy of AM 1/3 or have them copy the questions on page 6. Let them take turns asking and answering the questions, using the pictures on pages 4 and 5 for information.

(Continued on page 6.)

---

4. Analyze

a. Pairwork. Study these pictures and answer the questions on page 6.

Seven Forty-Five   Eight O'Clock   Nine Ten

Ten Thirty   Eleven Forty-Five   Twelve Thirty

One Ten   Two O'Clock   Two Fifty-Five

In homeroom

In the cafeteria

In English class
▲▲▲

In gym class

In science class

In history class

In art class

In math class

In the hallway

Activity 4: Analyze *(continued)*

6. *Part b.* To compare answers, have volunteers take turns asking and answering questions about Tran's schedule. Again warn them not to write anything in their books.

Activity 5: Write

1. *Part a.* Give pairs of students a copy of AM 1/4 or have them copy the chart on page 6. Read aloud the first sentence in the Language Focus box on page 6 and let students add the information to their chart. Have students complete the second sentence in the Language Focus box and add this information to the chart. Working in pairs, students can complete the chart, using the information on pages 4 and 5. Circulate to answer any questions.

2. *Part b.* Read aloud the question in the Language Focus box and let a student answer. Then let a volunteer ask a question about Tran's schedule.

3. Working in groups of four, students can compare charts by asking and answering questions about Tran's schedule. (Answers: second, art; third, math; fourth, gym; fifth, cafeteria; sixth, history; and seventh, science.)

Where is Tran at . . . . .

seven forty-five?	*in homeroom*
eight?	
nine ten?	
ten thirty?	
eleven forty-five?	
twelve thirty?	
one ten?	
two?	
two fifty-five?	

b. Compare answers with your classmates.

5. **Write**

a. Pairwork. Write Tran's class schedule in a chart like this. Use the information on pages 4–5.

Tran's Class Schedule		
Period	**Time**	**Class**
Homeroom	7:30–7:50	*homeroom*
First Period	7:55–8:50	*English*
Second Period	8:55–9:50	
Third Period	9:55–10:50	
Fourth Period	10:55–11:50	
Fifth Period	11:55–12:50	
Sixth Period	12:55–1:50	
Seventh Period	1:55–2:50	

Language Focus

■ Tran's first-period class is English.

■ Tran's second-period class is
_____ .

---

b. Compare answers with another pair.

A: What is Tran's _____-period class?

B: _____ .

6. Write

a. On your own. Write your schedule for today in a chart like this.

My Schedule		
Period	**Time**	**Class**
Homeroom		
First Period		
Second Period		
Third Period		
Fourth Period		
Fifth Period		
Sixth Period		
Seventh Period		

b. Pairwork. Compare schedules with a partner.

Language Focus

Q: What is Tran's first-period class?
A: English.

Language Focus

A: What is your first-period class?
B: English. What is your first-period class?
A: English.

Activity 6: Write

1. *Part a.* On the board, write your school schedule, using the chart on page 7 as a model. As you write, tell about your schedule.

2. Give each student a copy of AM 1/5. Have them write their schedule in the chart.

3. *Part b.* Work with a student partner to model this activity. Ask each other questions to compare schedules, using the model in the Language Focus box.

4. Put students in pairs to compare schedules.

Activity 7: Interview

1. *Part a.* Copy on the board the chart on page 8. Have students come to the board to add their names to the first column of the chart. Add your own name to the chart too.

2. Introduce the word *favorite* by pointing to each school subject and using gestures, facial expressions, and/or stars to indicate your preferences. Identify your favorite subject and add this information to the chart. For example, *My favorite class is history.*

3. *Part b.* Model the activity by asking a student: *What is your favorite class?* Encourage this student to ask you about your favorite class.

4. Put students in pairs to ask about their favorite class. Then have students add their partner's answer to the chart on the board.

7. **Interview**

a. Classwork. Add your name to a chart on the board.

Name	art	English	gym	history	math	music	science
Mei		✓					

Language Focus

Q: What is your favorite class?
A: Science.

b. Pairwork. Interview a partner. Add your partner's answer to the chart on the board.

A: What is your favorite class?

B: _____ . What is your favorite class?

A: _____ .

c. Classwork. Count your classmates' answers. Write
   the numbers in a chart like this:

Favorite Class	Number of Students
art	2
English	2
gym	3
history	1
math	4
music	2
science	3

d. Pairwork. Which class is the most popular? Which
   class is the least popular? Write your answers on a
   line like this:

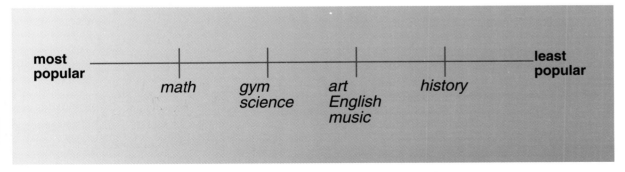

e. Compare charts with your classmates.

5. *Part c.* Have students count the number of checkmarks in each column of the chart on the board. Together transfer this information to a chart like the one on page 9.

6. *Part d.* Have students study the line chart on page 9. Show how it relates to the chart in part c.

7. Have pairs of students make their own line chart showing the range from most popular to least popular classes.

8. *Part e.* Have pairs post their line charts on a classroom wall. Together look for similarites and differences in the charts.

Activity 8: Explore Your School

1. Do this activity if your students are unfamiliar with the resources at your school. To complete the activity, students will need to take a tour of the school.

2. Together study the pictures on pages 10 and 11. More proficient students can tell what the people in the pictures are doing.

3. Give each student a copy of AM 1/6 (which is an expanded copy of the chart on page 11). Together think of other places to add to the chart. For example, *Does your school have a guidance office? Does your school have a principal's office?* Together answer the questions by circling *yes* or *no* in the *Before your trip* column of the chart.

4. Tour your school, looking for the places in your chart. More proficient students can tell what people are doing in each place.

5. After the trip, have students complete the chart, circling their answers in the *After your trip* column. Together compare answers before and after the tour.

8. **Explore Your School**

Classwork. Answer the questions on page 11. Then take a trip around your school and answer the questions again.

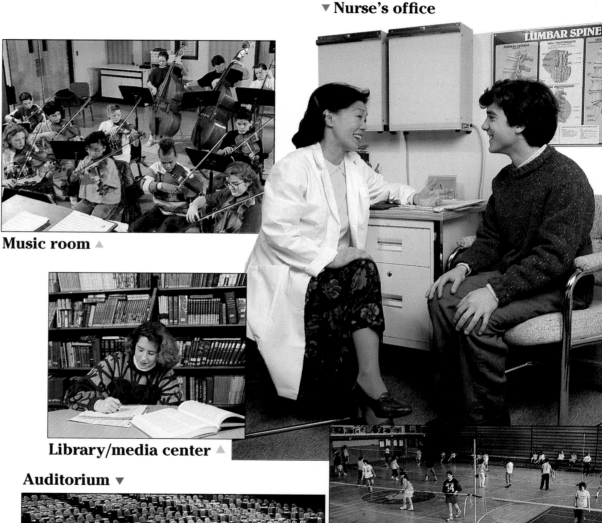

▼ **Nurse's office**

Music room ▲

Library/media center ▲

Auditorium ▼

Gym ▲

PLACES AT YOUR SCHOOL				
Questions	Answers			
	Before your trip		After your trip	
Does your school have an auditorium?	Yes	No	Yes	No
Does your school have a gym?	Yes	No	Yes	No
Does your school have an outdoor track?	Yes	No	Yes	No
Does your school have a woodshop?	Yes	No	Yes	No
Does your school have a library/media center?	Yes	No	Yes	No
Does your school have a cafeteria?	Yes	No	Yes	No
Does your school have a computer lab?	Yes	No	Yes	No
Does your school have a science lab?	Yes	No	Yes	No
Does your school have a nurse's office?	Yes	No	Yes	No
Does your school have a music room?	Yes	No	Yes	No
_____	Yes	No	Yes	No

Computer lab ▲

▼**Science lab**

Outdoor track ▲

▲ **Woodshop**

Activity 9: Recall

1. *Part a.* Together study the pictures on pages 12 and 13. Ask, *What are they doing? What is she doing? What is he doing?* Students can answer by reading the captions.

2. Put students in groups of 3 or 4. Provide each group with one copy of AM 1/6 or have them copy the chart on page 12. Students in a group can take turns asking questions and recording their partners' answers. Circulate to support less proficient students.

3. *Part b.* Have groups compare charts and report any differences.

9. **Recall**

a. Groupwork. On your trip around the school, did you see anyone doing these things? Where? Write your answers in a chart.

Writing ▼

▲ **Working in a group**

Playing basketball ▲

Reading ▲

Did you see anyone . . . ?	Yes	No	If yes, where?
reading			
writing			
working in a group			
writing on the blackboard			
standing in line			
playing basketball			
using a computer			

b. Compare charts with another group.

Using a computer ▲

▲ **Writing on the blackboard**

▲ **Standing in line**

Activity 10: Interview

1. *Part a.* Model this activity by interviewing a student partner. Ask the questions in the chart and record your partner's answers on AM 1/7. Then let your partner interview you and record your answers.

2. Put students in pairs, and give each student a copy of AM 1/7. Ask students to interview their partners and record the answers in their chart.

3. *Part b.* Model this activity by writing on the board several sentences about your partner's likes. For example, *My partner likes to play basketball.* Have students report one thing that their partner likes to do, using the model in the Language Focus box.

10. **Interview**

a. Pairwork. Interview your partner.

A: Do you like to ___read_____?
B: Yes I do. (No, I don't).

Do you like to _____?	Yes	No
read	✓	
play basketball		
work in a group		
write		
stand in line		
use a computer		

b. Tell the class about your partner.

My partner likes to _____.

Language Focus

Q: Do you lke to read?
A: Yes, I do. (No, I don't.)

Language Focus

▪ My partner likes to read.
▪ Mei likes to play basketball.

Activity Menu

Read the activities to the class and answer any questions. Then have students individually or in small groups select a project for a class or homework assignment. Projects can be shared with the class and/or displayed in the classroom.

Activity Menu

Choose one of the following activities to do.

1. Take Photographs
Take photographs of students in different places at your school. Ask your classmates to write captions for the photographs.

2. Draw a map
Draw a map of your school for new students. Choose important places at your school and locate them on your map.

3. Go on a Scavenger Hunt
Find these things at your school. Tell where you found each thing. Then compare ideas with your classmates.

These students are playing badminto the school gym.

What	Where
▪ a basketball hoop	*in the gym*
▪ a drinking fountain	
▪ a wall map	
▪ a microscope	
▪ a copy machine	
▪ an atlas (book of maps)	
▪ a flag	
▪ _____	

4. Make a Class Map

Where are your classmates from? Locate these countries on a world map. Use small flags, pins, or other markers to identify each person's native country.

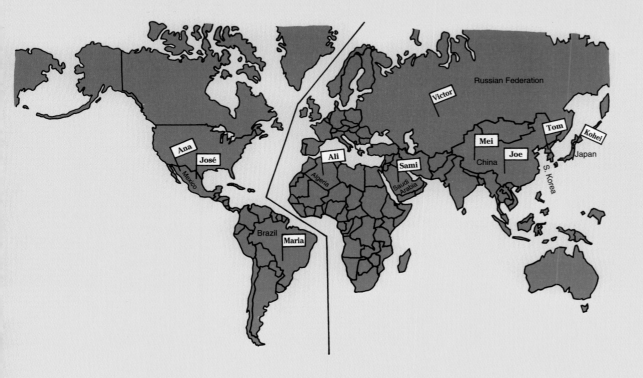

▼ Vacuum

Draw pictures ▶

Do homework ▼

▲ Do the dishes

Read ▶

▼ Play video games

Spending Free Time

▼ Take tests

Classwork. Add these activities to a chart like this.

School Activities	Housework	Free Time Activities
		play video games

▲ Ride a bike

▲ Read

◄ Cook

Student text pages 16–17

Activity 1: Classify

1. Introduce the pictures on pages 16–17 by asking questions about students' likes and dislikes. For example, *Leila, do you like to draw pictures?* Encourage volunteers to take turns asking and answering questions.

2. Draw on the board the chart from page 17. Have students find examples of school activities in the pictures and add them to the chart. Then ask them to find examples of housework and add them to the chart. Ask volunteers to write the remaining activities in the third column of the chart (Free Time Activities). Together study the examples of free time activities and come up with an explanation of this concept (fun things, things you choose to do).

3. Have students add more activities to each column in the chart. For ideas, students can look back at the pictures in Unit 1.

4. Extend this activity by asking students to collect pictures of people involved in different activities. Together write captions for the pictures, identifying the activities. Group the pictures (school activities, housework, free time activities) and post them on a classroom wall.

Activity 2: Listen

1. Introduce the free time activities on these pages by asking about students' likes and dislikes. For example, *Do you like to listen to music?* Then let students take turns asking each other questions.

2. Tell students that they will hear people talking about their free time activities. As they listen, they should find the picture of the person speaking. Play the tape and let students listen and point to each person.

3. Model the sentences in the Language Focus box by identifying things that you like to do in your free time. Write your ideas on the board. For example, *I like to play the guitar in my free time.*

4. Read aloud the question at the bottom of page 19 and let students write their answer on a piece of paper. Students can then report their answers in a chain activity. Start the game by saying: *I like to go shopping.* Then ask Student 1: *What do you like to do?* Student 1 answers and then asks another student: *What do you like to do?*

Language Focus

- I like to listen to music in my free time.
- I like to play soccer.
- I like to _____ .

2. Listen

Classwork. Listen and find the person.

Listen to music ▼

Play the guitar ▶

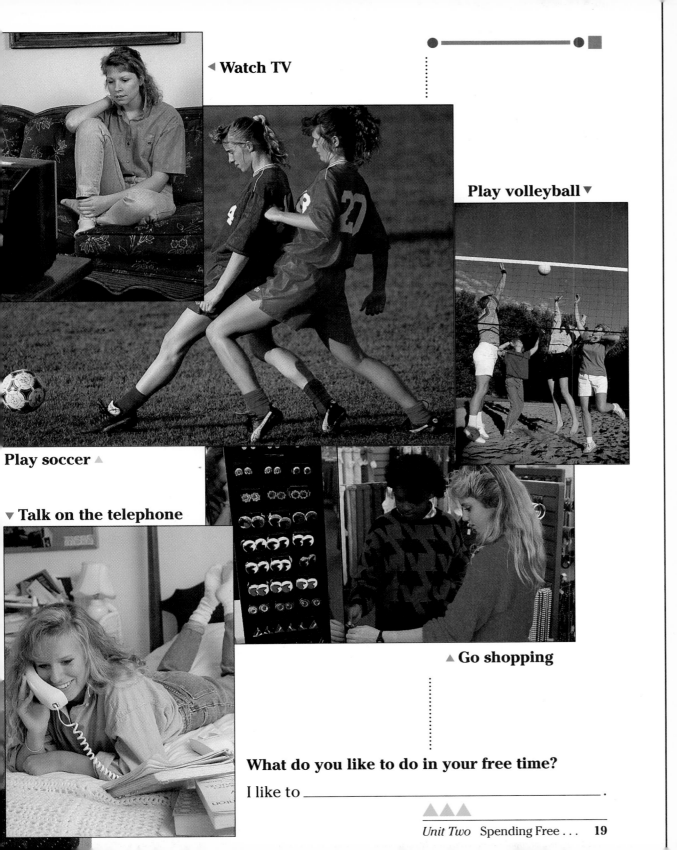

◄ **Watch TV**

Play volleyball ▼

Play soccer ▲

▼ **Talk on the telephone**

▲ **Go shopping**

What do you like to do in your free time?

I like to _____ .

Activity 3: Classify

1. *Part a.* Students can first study the pictures on page 20. Ask questions to find out who likes to play volleyball and who likes to ride a bike. For example, *Juan, do you like to play volleyball?*

2. Put students together in pairs and give each pair a copy of AM 2/1. Explain that *riding a bike* is an outdoor activity and *volleyball* is both an indoor and an outdoor activity. Have the pairs write these activities in the appropriate columns of their charts. Read aloud the list of activities at the top of page 20, and have pairs add them to their charts. When students have finished writing, the pairs can get together to compare their charts.

3. Choose one student to be your partner. Ask this student the two questions at the bottom of page 20: *What do you like to do outdoors? What do you like to do indoors?* Then let the student ask you the same two questions. Write your answers and your partner's answers on the board, using the model in the Language Focus box. For example, *I like to play soccer outdoors. My partner likes to ride a bike.* Next ask two volunteers to interview each other, using the same questions. Have them write their answers and their partner's answers on the board.

4. Have students work in pairs to answer the questions on page 20, writing their answers and their partner's answers on a piece of paper. On the reverse side of the paper have them write their name and their partner's name. Collect these papers, mix them up, and spread them on a table with the sentences showing. Without turning the papers over to read the names, have students look for papers that match. For example, paper 1 says: *I like to listen to music. My partner likes to draw.* Paper 2 says, *I like to draw. My partner likes to listen to music.* When they find a matching pair, have them check the reverse side to see if the names are the same.

(Continued on page 21.)

---

3. Classify

a. Pairwork. Put these activities into two groups. Then answer the questions below.

ride a bike	play soccer
play volleyball	draw
listen to music	play the guitar
go shopping	

Indoor/Outdoor Activities

play volleyball

Outdoor Activities

ride a bike

Language Focus

- I like to play soccer.
- My partner likes to ride a bike.

What do you like to do outdoors?

I like to . . . . .

My partner likes to . . . . .

What do you like to do indoors?

I like to . . . . .

My partner likes to . . . . .

b. Pairwork. Put these outdoor activities into two groups:

Swim ▶

Play baseball

Fish ▲

Ski ▲

Cold Weather Activities | **Hot Weather Activities**

Go to the beach ▲

What do you like to do in cold weather?

I like to . . . . .

My partner likes to . . . . .

What do you like to do in hot weather?

I like to . . . . .

My partner likes to . . . . .

5. *Part b.* Introduce the pictures on page 21 by asking students if they like to do these activities. For example, *Ali, Do you like to play baseball?*

6. Make a chart on the board with the headings *Cold Weather Activities* and *Hot Weather Activities.* Use the drawings on page 21 to clarify the concept of cold and hot weather. Ask, *Do you like to go to the beach in cold weather? Do you like to go to the beach in hot weather?* Have a volunteer write *go to the beach* in the appropriate column of the chart on the board.

7. Working in pairs, students draw a two-column chart on their paper and group the activities listed at the top of page 21, writing each in the appropriate column. Have pairs compare lists and discuss any differences of opinion. (Some activities, such as fishing, can be placed in both categories.)

8. Extend this activity by asking students to think of other hot and cold weather activities and add these to a chart on a large piece of paper. Display this chart and encourage students to keep adding to it and to find pictures to illustrate it. Help with unfamiliar vocabulary as needed.

9. Have students get together with a new partner to complete the sentences at the bottom of page 21, using a new piece of paper. If desired, you can follow the procedure suggested in Part a, step 4 with these new papers.

Activity 4: Play a Game

1. *Parts a–d.* Demonstrate the activity with a student partner. Draw 2 large rectangles on the board to represent index cards. Ask your partner: *What do you like to do in your free time?* Write your partner's name and answer in one of the rectangles. For example, *Jan likes to listen to music.* In the other rectangle, make a simple drawing of a radio or a person listening to music. Let your partner interview you and then write and illustrate your answer in two rectangles on the board.

2. Give each student 2 index cards. Working in pairs, students should interview their partners and complete the index cards, writing the partner's answer on one and drawing a picture to illustrate it on the other.

3. Put students in groups of 5 or 6 to play *Concentration.* Model the game by using one group's cards. Mix up the cards and place them face down as pictured in the text. Turn over two cards. If they match, remove them, put them in front of you, and take another turn. If they do not match, turn them over again. Let another student in your group turn over two cards. Let the class watch as this group plays the game. At the end of the game, the student with the most cards wins.

4. Let the groups play while you circulate in the classroom to answer any questions.

4. Play a Game

Materials: two index cards per student

a. Pairwork. Interview your partner.

   Q: What do you like to do in your free time?
   A: I like to _____*play the guitar*_____ .

b. Write your partner's answer on a card like this:

Marta likes to play the guitar

c. On another card, illustrate your partner's answer.

d. Get together in groups of 5 or 6. Follow your teacher's instructions to play a game called *Concentration.*

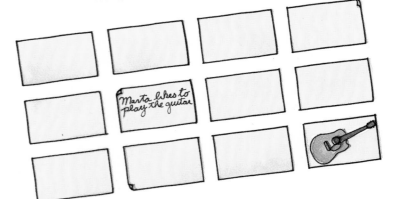

5. Interview

a. Classwork. Listen and record each person's answer in a chart like this.

Do you like to listen to music?	Yes, I do.	No, I don't.
Do you like to talk on the telephone?	Yes, I do.	No, I don't.
Do you like to play soccer?	Yes, I do.	No, I don't.
Do you like to go shopping?	Yes, I do.	No, I don't.
Do you like to watch TV?	Yes, I do.	No, I don't.

b. Pairwork. Interview a partner.

**Hang out with ▲
friends**
  Play basketball ▶

Go to the movies ▼

▲ Dance

Do you like to _____?	Yes, I do	No, I don't
play basketball	✓	
dance		
go to the movies		
hang out with friends		
_____		
_____		

> ### Language Focus
>
> **Q:** Do you like to play basketball?
> **A:** Yes, I do. (No, I don't.)

Activity 5: Interview

1. *Part a.* Give each student a copy of AM 2/2. Tell students that they will hear five questions and answers. They should circle the answer that they hear. Play the tape or read the script aloud. Play the tape again so that students can check their answers. Then have students compare answers. (Answers: Yes, I do. No, I don't. Yes, I do. No, I don't. Yes, I do.)

2. Extend the activity by having students ask and answer the questions in the chart. For example, *Do you like to listen to music? Yes, I do.*

3. *Part b.* Introduce the free time activities in the photographs by asking questions such as, *Who likes to dance?*

4. Model the activity by interviewing one student and completing the checklist. Then let the class interview you while one student records your answers.

5. Have students get together in pairs to interview each other. Encourage them to add other activities to the checklist on AM 2/2. Students will share their answers in the next part of the activity.

(Continued on page 24.)

Activity 5: Interview (continued)

6. *Part c.* Copy on the board the two diagrams. Have students take turns coming to the board to add their partner's name to the appropriate column in each diagram. Model the affirmative and negative forms of the present tense by reading aloud the information in the diagrams. For example, *Norio likes to dance. Sandra doesn't like to dance.* Then let students take turns reporting information from the diagrams.

7. Read the questions on page 24 aloud. Let students write the number of names in each category on the board. Together write sentences. For example, *Five students like to dance. Seven students don't like to dance.*

Activity 6: Interview

1. Model the activity by asking who likes or doesn't like to do the activities on the chart. For example, ask *Do you like to cook?* When a student answers *Yes,* write his or her name in the appropriate space on AM 2/3. Repeat with the second item on the chart.

2. Then give each student a copy of AM 2/3 or have them copy the chart in the book. Together add more likes and dislikes to the chart. For example, *Likes to fish.* Ask students to move around the classroom while they do this activity; discourage them from simply interviewing one student.

3. Have students take turns reporting information from their chart. For example, *Sam likes to run. Leila doesn't like to draw.*

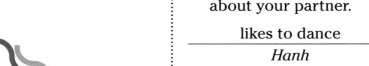

c. **Classwork.** Make a class chart. Add information about your partner.

likes to dance	doesn't like to dance
Hanh	*Carl*
Don	*Magda*

likes to play basketball	doesn't like to play basketball

Language Focus

- Hanh likes to dance.
- Carl doesn't like to dance.

How many students like to dance? _____
How many students don't like to dance? _____
How many students like to play basketball? _____
How many students don't like to play basketball? _____

6. **Interview**

On your own. Find someone who ___*likes to cook*___ .
Write the person's name in a chart like this.

Find someone who_____ .	
likes to cook	*Carl*
doesn't like to cook	*José*
likes to run	
doesn't like to swim	
likes to go to the beach	
doesn't like to draw	

Language Focus

A: Carl, do you like to cook?
B: Yes, I do.

A: José, do you like to cook?
C: No, I don't.

7. Compare

a. Pairwork. Ask your partner about free time activities. Together make a Venn Diagram like this:

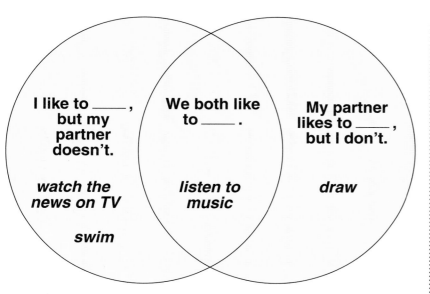

I like to _____, but my partner doesn't.

watch the news on TV

swim

We both like to _____ .

listen to music

My partner likes to _____, but I don't.

draw

Language Focus

A: Do you like to listen to music?

B: Sure. What about you?

A: I do, too.

B: Do you like to swim?

A: No, I don't. What about you?

B: I really like to swim.

b. Write several sentences about you and your partner.

I like to swim but my partner doesn't

We both like to listen to music.

Language Focus

- I like to swim, but Carlos doesn't.
- We both like to listen to music.
- Carlos likes to draw, but I don't.

Activity 7: Compare

1. *Part a.* Write *Free Time Activities* on the board and have students list a number of examples.

2. Put a large blank Venn Diagram on the board. Ask one student to be your partner. Take turns asking about the free time activities on the board, using the questions and answers in the upper Language Focus box. For example, ask each other *Do you like to watch TV?* If you both say *Yes,* write *Watch TV* in the center of the diagram. If you say *Yes* but your partner says *No,* write *Watch TV* on the left side of the diagram. If you say *No* and your partner says *Yes,* write *Watch TV* on the right side.

3. Tell about the information in your Venn Diagram. For example, *I like to swim but Jorge doesn't. We both like to go to the beach.* Leave your diagram on the board.

4. Let two volunteers make a Venn Diagram on the board, comparing likes and dislikes. Then give each student a copy of AM 2/4. Have them work in pairs to make their own Venn Diagrams. Circulate to answer questions.

5. *Part b.* Model the activity by writing several sentences on the board, based on your Venn Diagram. Use the sentences in the lower Language Focus box as models. For example, *We both like to dance. I like to cook but Jorge doesn't.* Encourage your partner to write several sentences, too.

6. Let students work on their own to write sentences on another piece of paper. Circulate to assist less proficient students as needed and to check students' work. Ask students to put their names on their paper, but not on their Venn Diagrams.

7. Post the Venn Diagrams on a wall. Collect the sentences and redistribute them. Then ask students to find the Venn Diagram that matches their sentences.

Activity 8: Invite

1. *Part a.* Read the dialogues in the Language Focus box with a student. Extend invitations to different students and let them accept or refuse your invitations. For example, *Do you want to play volleyball today? Do you want to go shopping?* Let volunteers invite you or another student to do something.

2. Together study the photographs on page 26 and read the captions. Tell students they will hear four short dialogues. They should listen and point to the person speaking. Play the tape or read the script.

3. *Part b.* Read the sample dialogues aloud with a volunteer. Then let pairs practice the dialogues, substituting other activities.

4. Have volunteers perform the dialogues for the class.

5. For additional practice, bring to class pictures of various free time activities. You will need two pictures of each activity for this game. Put the pictures on a table and have students go to the table one at a time and quickly choose a picture. Discourage them from showing their picture to other students. Their next task is to invite different classmates to do the activity in their picture. Students can accept an invitation only if their picture matches. If they have a different picture, they must politely refuse.

---

8. Invite

a. Classwork. Listen and find the person.

Sure. I'd love to.

I'd love to, but I'm busy.

Great idea.

Sorry, I can't.

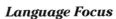

Language Focus

- **Q:** Do you want to play basketball?
- **A:** Sure. I'd love to.
- **Q:** Let's go shopping.
- **A:** I'd love to, but I'm busy.

b. Pairwork. Practice these dialogues.

A: Do you want to __play basketball__ ?
B: Sure. I'd love to. (Yes, I do. Great idea!)

A: Let's __go shopping__ .
B: I'd love to, but I'm busy. (Sorry I can't.)

9. Match

Pairwork. Choose words to complete the chant below.

▼ **Pole**

▲ **Net**

▲ **Brush**

◄ **Hoop**

▲ **Board**

◄ **Pen**

I'd Love To

I'd love to play basketball, but I don't have a _hoop_ .

I'd love to write a letter, but I don't have a . . . .

I'd love to go fishing, but I don't have a . . . .

I'd love to paint a picture, but I don't have a . . . .

I'd love to go surfing, but I don't have a . . . .

I'd love to play volleyball, but I don't have a . . . .

But I do have . . . , so let's . . . .

▲▲▲

Unit Two Spending Free . . . **27**

Activity 9: Match

1. Together, identify the equipment in the photographs. Encourage more proficient students to tell what the equipment is used for.

2. Read aloud the chant, saying *hmmm* for the missing words. For example, *I'd love to write a letter but I don't have a hmmm*. Keep a steady beat, four beats for each line, with emphasis on the syllables with dots over them.

3. Divide the class into small groups or pairs. Give each group or pair one copy of AM 2/5. Let them work together to complete the sentences and then practice reading the sentences aloud as a chant (but softly so as not to disturb the other groups or pairs). For example, they can read the chant as a group, take turns reading a line or clause, or start reading quietly and build to a crescendo.

4. Let each group read its chant to the class.

5. Play the tape and let students listen to one version of the chant.

6. Encourage more proficient students to write a new chant with different activities and equipment.

▲▲▲ **27**

Activity 10: Shared Reading

1. Write the word *hobby* on the board. Have students look at the pictures on pages 28 and 29 and identify these hobbies (playing chess, building a submarine, collecting stamps, painting pictures). List them on the board. Identify any unfamiliar things in the pictures (chessboard, chess pieces, submarine, stamps, magnifying glass, jar, etc.) and list them on the board. Encourage students to ask you about things in the pictures. For example, *What's this? It's a tube of paint.*

2. Read the instruction line aloud. Then play the tape or read the information aloud. Have students find New York and Florida on a map. Then ask different students: *Do you like to play chess? Do you like to build things?* Let more proficient students tell about the two hobbies, based on the information in the reading and their own experience.

10. Shared Reading

A hobby is something you do for fun. What are these people's hobbies?

Chess is popular at Junior High School 43 in Harlem, New York. Every day at lunch time, students get together to play chess. After school, some of the students play for three or four more hours.

Stephen Barton, a high school student in Hernando Beach, Florida, likes to build things—big things. He spent hundreds of hours at the computer and in the library, learning about submarines. Then he built this submarine in his basement.

11. Evaluate

Groupwork. Evaluate the hobbies in the reading. Tell what you think. Then add other hobbies to a chart like this.

Really Interesting Very Interesting Great ***	Interesting Fun **	Okay All right *	Boring —
building a submarine		chess	

Language Focus

- Chess is okay.
- _____ is boring.

Painting pictures

Collecting stamps

Activity 11: Evaluate

1. Together study the chart on page 29. Use the stars in the chart and body language to explain the four evaluation categories. List these hobbies on the board: *playing chess, building a submarine, collecting stamps, painting pictures, fishing, playing the guitar.* Show how you might evaluate these hobbies by listing them in a chart on the board. Think out loud as you write. For example, *I think playing chess is fun. Collecting stamps is boring.* Then erase the hobbies so that students aren't tempted to copy your opinions.

2. Put students in groups and have each group make a copy of the chart. Let them work together to evaluate hobbies. Encourage them to agree on an answer.

3. If possible, bring in pictures showing people involved in different types of hobbies. Let students add these to their evaluation chart.

4. Let the groups report their ideas to the class. For example, *Chess is very interesting. Collecting stamps is okay.*

Activity 12: Make a Cluster Diagram

Together collect information about one of the hobbies on the previous page by making a cluster diagram on the board. Students can share information from the reading and their own experience. You can act as a consultant, helping with unfamiliar words. More proficient students might want to make a cluster diagram for each hobby and then compare them.

Activity 13: Write

Part a. In this activity, students can write about a hobby of their choice. Have them first collect information on a cluster diagram. They might also get information by talking to you or other students in the class.

Part b. Students can use their cluster diagram to tell a classmate about their hobby.

Part c. Give students time in class to write about their hobby. Provide less proficient students with a structured model to follow:

Chess

My hobby is chess. You need a chessboard and chess pieces to play. You need a good memory too. You can play chess at home and at school. Chess is fun.

Part d. Have students choose a way to publish their work. For example, they might want to make a wall chart of hobbies, using their writing and illustrations. They could also make copies of their writing and put them together to make a class book.

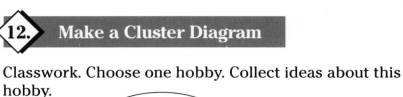

12. Make a Cluster Diagram

Classwork. Choose one hobby. Collect ideas about this hobby.

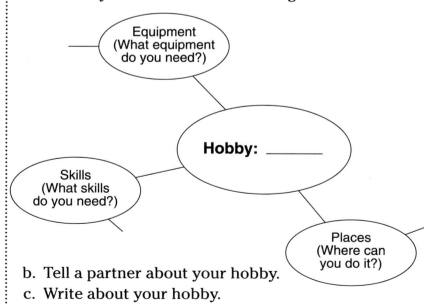

13. Write

On your own. Tell about one of your hobbies.

a. Collect your ideas in a cluster diagram like this.

b. Tell a partner about your hobby.
c. Write about your hobby.
d. Share your writing with your classmates.

14. Read a Chart

a. **Classwork.** Read this chart and tell about Nina Todisco's daily schedule.

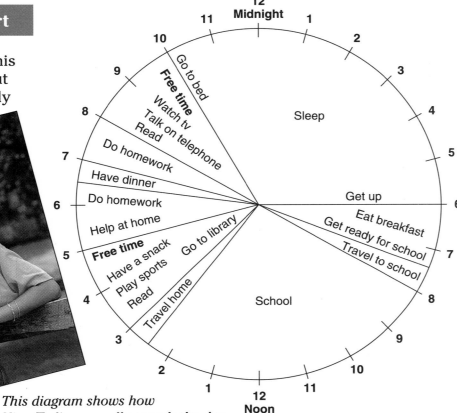

This diagram shows how Nina Todisco usually spends the day.

b. **On your own. Complete these sentences.**

Nina . . . . at six o'clock in the morning.

She leaves home at . . . . .

She gets to school at . . . . .

School ends at . . . . .

After school, she . . . . .

At . . . . , she has dinner.

After dinner, she . . . . .

At ten o'clock in the evening, she . . . . .

She has some free time in the afternoon between

. . . . . and . . . . .

Language Focus

- She gets up at 6.
- She leaves home at 7:30.

Activity 14: Read a Chart

1. *Part a.* Depending on the language abilities of your students, you may want to first review time expressions and introduce vocabulary related to everyday routines. On the board, list several things you do every day (get up, eat breakfast, leave for school, eat lunch, do housework, eat dinner, go to bed). Next to each activity draw a clock showing the time you usually do these daily activities. For example, *get up* (with a clock showing 6 o'clock). Then tell students about your daily schedule. For example, *I get up at 6 o'clock.* Have a volunteer come to the board and draw clocks showing when he or she does the activities listed on the board. Have the class work together to tell about this student's daily activities. For example, *Ahmed gets up at 7.*

2. Together study the 24-hour circle diagram on page 31. Introduce the words *between, after, from, to,* and *at* by using them in sentences about Nina Todisco's schedule. For example, *Nina has some free time **between** 3 and 5. She has dinner **from** 6 **to** 6:30. **After** dinner, she does her homework.* Then let students tell about Nina's schedule. If they neglect to use the third person singular form of the verb, simply restate the information correctly. For example, *That's right. Nina eats breakfast at 6.* For additional clarification, make a chart on the board showing the first person and third person forms of the verbs.

I	She/He
eat	eats
have dinner	has dinner

Part b. Students can work on their own to write sentences on another piece of paper. Have pairs compare answers and then let students take turns reading the sentences aloud to the class. Play the tape and let students listen and check their sentences.

(Continued on page 32.)

Activity 14: Read a Chart *(continued)*

Part c. Ask a volunteer to read the questions aloud. Students can then write their answers on another piece of paper. Have pairs compare answers and then report to the class.

Activity 15: Write

1. *Parts a and b.* Give each student a copy of AM 2/6. Students should first complete the sentences telling about their daily schedules. They can then use these sentences to complete the 24-hour circle diagram.

(Continued on page 33.)

She has some free time in the evening between ..... and .....

c. On your own. Answer these questions.

How much free time does Nina Todisco have each day?

What does she do in her free time?

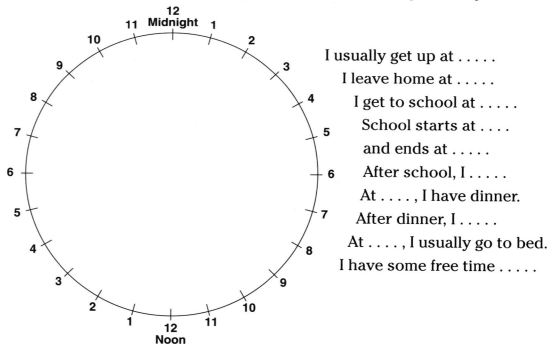

⟨15.⟩ **Write**

a. On your own. Write about your daily schedule.

I usually get up at . . . . .
I leave home at . . . . .
I get to school at . . . . .
School starts at . . . .
and ends at . . . . .
After school, I . . . . .
At . . . . , I have dinner.
After dinner, I . . . . .
At . . . . , I usually go to bed.
I have some free time . . . . .

b. Draw a circle diagram. Show your daily schedule.

c. Exchange circle diagrams with a partner. Write about your partner's schedule.

My partner gets up at 6:30.

16. **Chant**

a. Classwork. Listen to the chant.

The Nothing to Do Blues

Hey man, I'm feeling blue.
There's nothing at all for me to do.

Play ball. Read a book.
What do you mean there's nothing to do?

---

b. Pairwork. Add your own words to the chant.

Nothing to Do

Hey man, I'm feeling blue.
There's nothing at all for me to do.

——————— . ——————— .

What do you mean there's nothing to do?

c. Read your chant to the class.

2. *Part c.* Model Part c by choosing one student's circle diagram and writing sentences about it on the board. Then have students exchange diagrams and write about their partner's schedule. Encourage them to ask their partners questions if they want additional information.

3. Let students take turns telling about their partner's schedule.

4. Post the circle diagrams and have students look for similarities and differences in their classmates' daily routines.

Activity 16: Chant

1. *Part a.* Play the tape or read the chant aloud. Use the illustration on this page to explain the meaning of the expression *feeling blue.* If you read the chant aloud, use a steady beat, four beats per line, with emphasis on the syllables in **boldface** type below:

> **Hey, man,** I'm **feel**ing **blue.**
> There's **no**thing at **all** for **me** to **do.**
>
> **Play ball, read** a **book.**
> **What** do you **mean,** there's **no**thing to **do?**

2. Divide the class into two groups to read the chant aloud. Have them take turns reading a stanza.

3. *Parts b and c.* Have students work in small groups or pairs to write new lines for the chant. They can then read their chant aloud to the class. You may want to tape record their chants for playback later.

Activity Menu

Read the activities to the class and answer any questions. Then have students individually or in small groups select a project for a class or home-work assignment. Projects can be shared with the class and/or displayed in the classroom.

Activity Menu

Choose one of the following activities to do.

1. What do you do in your free time?
For one day, write down everything you do in your free time. Record your notes on a schedule like this:

2. No School Today
What do you do on Saturday? Make a chart showing how you spend the day. Show how much free time you have. Tell what you do in your free time.

3. Interview
Ask three people—your friends or people in your family—about their free time. Ask: *What do you like to do in your free time? What don't you like to do in your free time?* Record their answers in a chart like this:

Name	Likes to do	Doesn't like to do

Write a summary of what you learned.

4. Make a Collage of Hobbies
Tell your classmates about one of your hobbies. Bring materials from home to show what you do. Then make a class collage of hobbies. Include information and pictures about each person's hobby.

5. Is It Dangerous?

Collect pictures of different sports.
Evaluate each sport like this:

	Sports	
	bungee jumping	*tennis*
Very dangerous	✓	
Somewhat dangerous		
Slightly dangerous		
Not dangerous at all		

6. Play a Game

Teach your classmates how to play a card game or a board game like checkers.

7. Compare Daily Schedules

Compare your daily schedule with a partner's. Make a Venn Diagram like this:

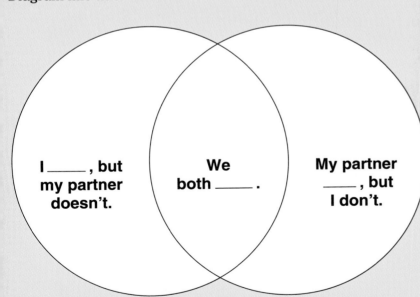

I _____, but my partner doesn't.

We both _____.

My partner _____, but I don't.

Counting Dollars and Cents

▲ .25
**Twenty-five cents
A quarter**

▲ .10
**Ten cents
A dime**

▲ .05
**Five cents
A nickel**

▲ .01
**One cent
A penny**

1. ▶ Listen

Classwork. Listen and find the amount of money.

▲ **$1.00**
One dollar

▲ **$5.00**
Five dollars

▲ **$10.00**
Ten dollars

▲ **$20.00**
Twenty dollars

Student text pages 36–37

Activity 1: Listen

1. Together look over the pictures of United States coins and bills. Point to each picture and say the amount. Students can repeat the amounts after you.

2. Point to a picture and ask, *How much is it?* Let students read the amount.

3. Tell students to point to the correct coin or bill as they listen. Read the script or play the tape.

4. Bring in various coins and bills, and let students identify the amounts.

5. With more proficient learners, ask about the woman in the top left picture: *What is the woman doing?* (Getting money from an ATM machine.) Ask, *Where do people keep large amounts of money?* (In a bank.) *What is a bank book for?* (To show how much money someone has saved in that bank.)

6. Give groups of students several coins. Have them find the numbers under the head of the person pictured on the coin. Ask, *What do you think these numbers tell?* (The year the coin was made.) Discuss the fact that some people collect coins and like to have, for example, one coin from every year that a coin of a particular design was made.

Activity 2: Identify

1. Model the activity, using box #1 as an example. Together count the one dollar bills in the box: *one, two, three, four, five.* Ask: *How much money is it?* (five dollars)

2. Give pairs of students a copy of AM 3/1 or draw the chart below on the board and have students copy it. Pairs should then write the amounts of money in the eight boxes on pages 38 and 39 in both numbers and words.

	Numbers	Words
1	$5.00	five dollars
2		
3		
4		
5		
6		
7		
8		

3. Have pairs get together in groups of four to compare answers. Then have groups report their answers to the class. (Answers: 1. five dollars; 2. thirty dollars; 3. twenty-five cents; 4. ten cents; 5. twenty-five cents; 6. five cents; 7. one dollar; 8. ten cents.)

2. Identify

Pairwork. How much money is in each box? Write the amounts.

1

2

3

4

5

6

7

8

Activity 3: Listen

1. *Part a.* Depending on the level of your class, you may want to first review the numbers 1–10. Ask students to hold up five fingers, eight fingers, etc. Let the class practice counting off, using the numbers 1–10.

2. Read the numbers in the box across each row, and let students repeat after you. Then read a number and have students point to it. Write numbers on the board, and let volunteers read them aloud.

3. Play the tape and have students point to the numbers as they hear them. (They will hear them first as they are in the box, then some numbers in random order.)

4. *Part b.* Write the pairs of numbers on the board as shown on page 40. Point to the numbers in each pair as you read them aloud. Students can repeat after you.

5. Have students copy these pairs of numbers. Then ask them to listen and circle the number they hear. Say *thirty,* and have them show which word they circled. Repeat with the word *fourteen*.

6. Read the script or play the tape. Give students time to circle the numbers. Read the script again or play the tape again and let students check their answers. Then have two pairs write their answers on the board so that the class can compare.

7. If more practice is needed, write the pairs of numbers on the board in numerals rather than words (13, 30, etc.). Read a number aloud and let volunteers point to the number they heard.

8. Hand out Monopoly money (or other play money), asking students if they want thirteen or thirty dollars, fourteen or forty etc. Give them the amount they ask for.

9. Play a sequencing game. Say a series of two numbers (e.g., *16, 17*), pause, and then let a volunteer add the third number in the series (18). That student can then start a new series.

(Continued on page 41.)

3. Listen

a. Classwork. Listen and find the number.

0 zero	1 one	2 two	3 three	4 four	5 five	6 six	7 seven
8 eight	9 nine	10 ten	11 eleven	12 twelve	13 thirteen	14 fourteen	15 fifteen
16 sixteen	17 seventeen	18 eighteen	19 nineteen	20 twenty	21 twenty-one	22 twenty-two	
30 thirty	40 forty	50 fifty	60 sixty	70 seventy	80 eighty	90 ninety	
100 one hundred		1000 one thousand					

b. Classwork. Listen and find the number.

thirteen	thirty
fourteen	forty
fifteen	fifty
sixteen	sixty
seventeen	seventy
eighteen	eighty
nineteen	ninety

4. Match

Pairwork. Find these amounts of money on page 41.

1. Five dollars and fifteen cents.

2. Two dollars and thirty cents.

3. Three dollars and fifty cents.

4. Fifty-seven cents.

5. One dollar and eighty cents.

6. Twenty-six cents.

Activity 4: Match

1. Bring to class an assortment of quarters, dimes, nickels, and pennies. Be sure there are several of each denomination. Give each student one coin. Tell students to find the other people in the class with the same coin. For example, all the people with dimes should get together, all those with nickels should get together, etc. There will be some disorder as students figure out how to get together, but let them work it out; (it's okay to show their coins). When the groups are together, have them figure out how much money the group has altogether. Then retrieve the coins.

2. Give each group different assortments of coins and have them figure out the total amount. Have them group their coins into piles of 25 cents each; (they may have an odd pile at the end). Again retrieve the coins.

3. Give each group different combinations of monopoly or play money to practice counting larger amounts.

4. Let pairs work together to match the written amounts on page 40 with the pictures on page 41. Have them write their answers on another piece of paper. Then have pairs compare answers. (Answers: 1. c; 2. b; 3. e; 4. f; 5. a; 6. d)

5. For additional practice with less proficient students, try this chain activity. Provide a "bank" with a five-dollar bill and several one-dollar bills. Include several quarters, nickels, dimes, and pennies. Tell Student 1 to give Student 2 a certain amount (e.g., $4.37). Student 2 accepts the money and checks to see if it is the correct amount. Direct Student 2 to give Student 3 a different amount, and so on.

Activity 5: Listen

1. Set the scene for this activity by asking about the picture at the top of the page: *Where are the people? What are they doing?*

2. Read the sample dialogue aloud with one student.

3. Together look over the pictures and let students guess the price of each item.

4. Review the correct way to write prices. On the board, write $20.99, $10.00, $ .50 and 50¢. Point out the correct place for the dollar sign and cent sign. Remind them not to use the two signs together.

5. On a piece of paper, each student should list the six items shown on this page. Tell them they will hear six short dialogues. They should listen and write the price of each item. Play the tape or read the dialogues aloud. Repeat the dialogues (or play the tapes, on which the dialogues are repeated) and let students check their answers.

6. Have students compare answers by acting out scenes at a store. They can ask about the prices of the pictured items, using the dialogues as a model. (Answers: dictionary, $12.95; Walkman, $25.00; watch, $35.00; backpack, $17.50; pen, $.55; calculator, $9.95.)

5. Listen

Classwork. Listen and write the price.

A: Excuse me. How much does this dictionary cost?
B: Twelve dollars and ninety-five cents.
A: Thanks.

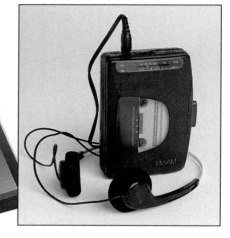

> ### Language Focus
>
> **Q:** How much does this dictionary cost?
> **A:** Twelve dollars and ninety-five cents.

Dictionary   **Walkman**   **Watch**

Backpack   **Pen**   **Calculator**

6. Guess

Groupwork. How much do you think these items cost? Write your guess in a chart.

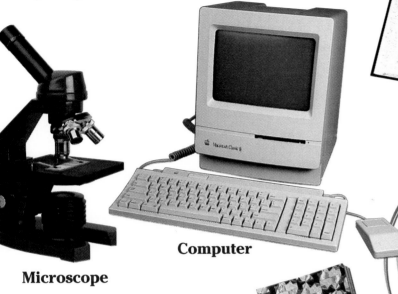

Microscope

Computer

Dictionary

Eraser

Notebook

Globe

Item	Price	
	Guess	**Actual**
microscope		
computer		
dictionary		
eraser		
notebook		
globe		

b. Compare your guesses with the actual prices on page 59.

Language Focus

- I think the notebook costs about one dollar.
- We think the microscope costs five hundred dollars.

Activity 6: Guess

1. Have students identify the items in the pictures and tell what people do with these things.

2. Model the activity by working with one student to guess the price of a microscope. As you discuss the price of the microscope, write down any unfamiliar words that come up in your discussion. For example, *That's too much. That's not enough.*

3. Put students in groups of 3 or 4 and give each group a copy of AM 3/2. Have students work together to guess the price of each item. They should write their guesses in the appropriate column in the chart. Make a master chart on the board and let each group report its guesses, using the model in the Language Focus box.

4. To check their guesses, pairs of students can act out scenes at a store. One student goes to the store and asks about the price of an item. Another student looks at the prices of these items at the bottom of page 59 and answers. The groups should write this amount in the appropriate column in their chart. Have the class decide which group made the closest guess for the price of each item.

5. Extend this activity by bringing in catalogs and store flyers. Have each student choose an item to show to the class. Let the rest of the class first guess the price and then compare guesses with the actual price.

6. If feasible, take the class to the school bookstore. Tell them to bring money to buy something (pencil, ruler, eraser, folder, etc.) Devise a simple dialogue and practice beforehand.

Activity 7: Compare

1. Introduce comparatives, using the pictures in the Language Focus box. Ask: *Which is cheaper, the baseball or the soccer ball?* Let a volunteer read the answer aloud. Be sure students understand the concept "cheaper."

2. Ask about the items in Activity 6 on page 43. For example, *Which is cheaper, the computer or the microscope?* Let volunteers ask about the items on page 42.

3. Together identify the pictured items on pages 44 and 45. Then read the question in the chart, adding the first items: *Which is cheaper, the basketball or the soccer ball?* Let the class guess the cheaper item.

4. Give pairs of students a copy of AM 3/3. They should circle their guesses in this chart. Have pairs take turns reporting their guesses. For example, *We think the music cassette is cheaper.* (Students will find out the actual prices of these items in the next activity.)

---

7. Compare

Pairwork. Which is cheaper? Circle your guesses in a chart like this.

Which is cheaper, the _____	or the _____ ?
1. basketball	soccer ball
2. ice skates	roller blades
3. music CD	music cassette
4. shampoo	toothpaste
5. roll of film	blank videotape
6. 19" color TV	VCR

Language Focus

Q: Which is cheaper, the baseball or the soccer ball?
A: The baseball.

Baseball $7.50

Soccer ball $24.95

▲ **Basketball**   ▲ **Soccer ball**

▼ **Roller blades**

Ice skates ▲

▲ Music CD

▲ Music cassette

Roll of film

▲ Blank videotape

Shampoo ▲

▲ Toothpaste

◄ 19"
color TV

▲ VCR

Activity 8: Collect Information

1. Have the pairs from Activity 7 work together again for this activity. Identify one person in each pair as "Student A" and the other as "Student B." Tell the Student A's to look only at pages 46 and 47. Tell the Student B's to turn to pages 48 and 49.

2. Make a chart like this on the board. Have students copy the chart and add the names of the twelve items pictured in the text.

Item	Price
basketball	
ice skates	

3. Model the activity by taking the role of a Student A. Ask a Student B: *How much does the basketball cost?* This student can find the answer on page 48. Write the student's answer in the chart on the board. Then have Student B ask you a question: *How much does the soccer ball cost?* Look for the answer on page 47. Let this student write your answer on his or her chart.

4. Pairs can work together to find the price of each item while you circulate to monitor the activity. Discourage students from looking at their partner's pages.

5. Have students look back at their charts on AM 3/3, count the number of correct guesses, and report to the class.

6. Write this sentence on the board: *The soccer ball is cheaper than the basketball.* Then have students tell about the items in their chart, using the model sentence on the board.

(Continued on page 48.)

---

8. Collect Information

Pairwork. Student A looks at pages 46 and 47 only. Student B looks at pages 48 and 49 only.

Student A: Ask your partner questions about these items. Write your partner's answers.

Example: *Student A: How much does the basketball cost?*
Student B: ___$29.99___ .

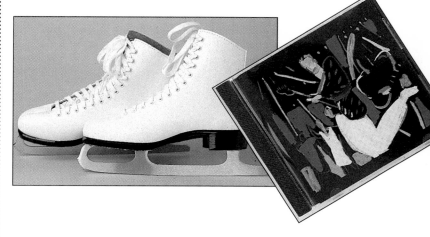

Student A: Answer your partner's questions about these items.

Example: *Student B: How much does a soccer ball cost?*
Student A: ___$24.95___ .

___$24.95___   ___$129.95___   ___$8.00___

___$1.99___   ___$7.00___   ___$299.00___

Now check your guesses from Activity #7.

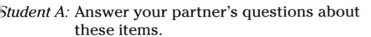

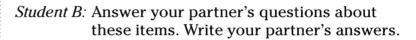

Student B: Answer your partner's questions about these items. Write your partner's answers.

Example: *Student A: How much does the basketball cost?*
Student B: ___$29.99___ .

$29.99

$75.50

$13.00

$2.99

$4.55

$325.00

Student B: Ask your partner about these items.

Example: *Student B: How much does a soccer ball cost?*
     Student A: ___$24.95___ .

Now check your guesses from Activity #7.

Activity 9: Compare

1. Give students time to look over the labeled pictures of different foods. Find out about their food likes and dislikes. For example, *Do you like hot dogs? Do you like to eat pizza?*

2. Ask about the price of each food. For example, *How much does a hamburger cost?*

3. Model the comparative form *more expensive* by reading the question in the Language Focus box. Q: *Which is more expensive, a hot dog or a hamburger?* Let a volunteer read the answer. Be sure the students understand the concept "more expensive."

4. Have students compare prices by answering the question under each picture.

5. Extend the activity by modeling additional questions, using the pictures. For example, *Which is more expensive, a salad or a piece of pizza?* Let volunteers ask questions too.

Language Focus

A: Which is more expensive, a hot dog or a hamburger?
B: A hamburger.

Small soda $.89

Small glass of milk $.79

Which is more expensive, a small soda or a small glass of milk?

9. Compare

Classwork. Compare the prices of these foods.

Hot dog $1.50   Hamburger $2.75

Which is more expensive, a hot dog or a hamburger?

Pizza $1.25   Taco $1.50

Which is more expensive, a slice of pizza or a taco?

Salad $2.95   Peanut butter sandwich $1.75

Which is more expensive, a salad or a peanut butter sandwich?

10. Listen

Classwork. Listen and write the total amount of each order.

A: I'd like a _hamburger and a small soda_ , please.

B: That will be $ _____ .

Order	Total Amount
hamburger small soda	
taco small glass of milk	
salad hot dog small soda	
peanut butter sandwich glass of water	

11. Roleplay

Pairwork. Practice ordering from this menu.

MENU
***
Hamburger................$2.70

Hot Dog................$1.55

Taco................$1.50

Peanut Butter Sandwich....$1.75

Pizza (1 slice)................$ .99

***

Salad................$1.95

***

Coffee...small..$.75, large....$.90

Soda.....small..$.89, large....$.99

Milk.......small..$.79, large....$.89

Activity 10: Listen

1. Use the picture to set the scene for this activity. Ask: *Where are these people? What is the man on the left doing? Do you like to eat out? Do you like to go to restaurants?*

2. Read the sample dialogue aloud. Let the class find the cost of the meal, using the information on page 50.

3. Hand out copies of AM 3/4. Tell students they will hear four short dialogues. In each dialogue a person is ordering a meal. They should write the cost of each meal. Play the tape or read the dialogues aloud. Let students listen to the dialogues again to check their answers; (the dialogues are repeated on the tape).

4. Ask pairs of students to practice the dialogue, using the prices they wrote down. See if the class agrees. (Answers: $3.64, $2.29, $5.34, and $1.75.)

Activity 11: Roleplay

1. Set up a restaurant in your classroom. This could be something as simple as a counter in a fast food restaurant. Let students take turns roleplaying a customer and a cashier, using the menu on this page. Introduce some humor by roleplaying an indecisive customer.

2. Extend the activity by having groups of students make up new menus with foods that they like and the prices. Let each group open a restaurant and take their classmates' orders.

Language Focus

A: I'd like _____ .
B: That'll be _____ .
That'll = That will

Activity 12: Play a Game

Materials:

two coins for each group (see step 4), different "markers" for each student in a group (e.g., different colored beans, small stones, tiny pieces of colored paper, etc.)

1. Write the words *deposit* and *withdraw* on the board. Demonstrate *depositing (adding)* and *withdrawing (subtracting or taking out)* money by role-playing scenes at a bank.

2. Tell students they are going to play a game in which they will deposit and withdraw money from the bank. Have them look at Your Bank Savings Account on page 53. Draw the chart on the board and show what happens to the balance when you withdraw or subtract money. Let students practice depositing and withdrawing money, using the chart on the board to record the transactions.

3. Demonstrate the concept of *heads* and *tails* by tossing two coins and reporting the results. For example, *Two heads.* Repeat several times. Have students in the class take turns tossing two coins and reading the results.

4. Put students in groups of three or four to play the game. Give each group a copy of AM 3/5 with the game board on it. Model the game by playing with two students while the rest of the class gathers around to watch. Explain that they must get from the Start circle to the Bank at the bottom of the page. Toss two coins and read the results. Have students look at the game rules on page 53 to interpret your roll. For example, if you got two heads, you can move two spaces. Make your move on the game board. Read the information in the square and make the appropriate deposit or withdrawal from your savings account on AM 3/6. Note that each person begins the game with $200 in his or her savings account. Then have one of your partners toss the coins, make a move, and record the deposit or withdrawal from his or her savings account. As you play, clarify any unfamiliar words on the game board. Continue until students understand the game.

(Continued on page 53.)

12. Play a Game

Groupwork. Read the game rules on page 53 and l[isten] to your teacher's instructions.

START →

You lost your wallet. Withdraw $10.00 from your savings account.	You babysat for a neighbor's child. Add $15.00 to your savings account.	You bought a [new] pair of blue jea[ns] Withdraw $25.[
A relative gave you some money. Deposit $10.00.	You lost a library book. Withdraw $20.00.	You bought a [new] radio. Subtract $30.00.
You went to a movie. Withdraw $7.00.	You need a new pair of sneakers. Withdraw $35.00.	You won a writ[ing] contest. Depos[it] $50.00.
You found some money on the street. Deposit $10.00.	You want to take guitar lessons. Withdraw $60.00.	You bought a present for a friend. Subtract $20.00.
You bought some school supplies— notebooks, pens, etc. Withdraw $10.00.	You painted a neighbor's kitchen. Add $40.00.	You bought a basketball. Subtract $30.0[
You went to the dentist. Withdraw $50.00.	You sold your old bicycle. Deposit $25.00.	You bought a u[sed] bicycle. Withdr[aw] $50.00.

B.[

Game Rules

 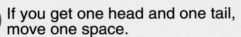
Take turns tossing two coins.
If you get two heads, move two spaces.

 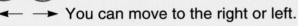
If you get one head and one tail,
move one space.

 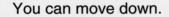
If you get two tails, lose a turn. Don't move.

 You can move to the right or left.

You can move down.

You can move one space to the right or left
and then one space down.

You cannot move up.
You cannot move diagonally.

Start the game with $200.00 in your savings account.
Write your deposits and withdrawals on a chart.
Add or subtract to find the balance.

Example:

Your Bank Savings Account

Date	Deposits (Add)	Withdrawals (Subtract)	Balance
2/15/93	+$200.00		$200.00
2/21/93		-$25.00	$175.00
2/23/93	+$25.00		$200.00

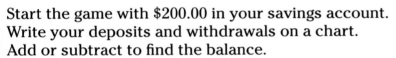

$$\begin{array}{r} \$200.00 \\ -25.00 \\ \hline \$175.00 \end{array}$$

$$\begin{array}{r} \$175.00 \\ +25.00 \\ \hline \$200.00 \end{array}$$

How much money do you have in your bank account at
the end of the game?

Activity 12: Play a Game *(continued)*

5. Give each student a copy of AM 3/6 or let them copy the Savings Account chart on page 53. Each time they move on the game board, they should record the deposit or withdrawal and the new balance. Another student can check their addition or subtraction.

6. Let students play the game. Circulate to answer any questions. At the end of the game have each student tell how much money is in his or her bank account.

7. As a follow-up activity, get some blank deposit/withdrawal forms from a local bank and have students practice completing the authentic forms.

Activity 13: Shared Reading and Writing

1. Read aloud the question at the top of the page: *What did people first use as money?* Let students make predictions, using the pictures on this page for ideas. (bricks of tea, shells, cows, fish hooks, beads) List their ideas on the board.

2. Read the paragraph aloud. Then have students add other ideas to the list on the board. Have students locate the places mentioned in the reading, using a world map or a globe. Answer any questions they have about vocabulary.

3. Have groups work together to list answers to the questions at the bottom of the page. (Possible answers: 1. easier to carry, smaller, lasts a long time, limited supply; 2. charge cards, checks.) Let groups compare answers.

4. Extend this activity by showing students examples of personal checks. You might, for example, bring in some cancelled checks for students to study.

5. Encourage interested students to find out more about the history of money by looking up this topic in an encyclopedia.

13. Shared Reading and Writing

What Did People First Use as Money?

Thousands of years ago, people didn't have coins and paper money. They used other things to buy and sell goods. In parts of Africa, Asia, and Australia, people used cowrie shells for money. In Mongolia, people used bricks of tea. In other parts of the world, people used things like salt, beads, cows, stones, fish hooks, and feathers.

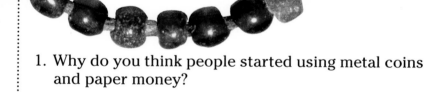

1. Why do you think people started using metal coins and paper money?

2. Besides coins and paper money, what do people use for money today?

14. Match

a. Pairwork. Look at some money from different countries. Complete a chart like this.

What Do You See on the Money?

Country	Words	Numbers	Person	Building	Other
Germany	✔	✔			✔

▲ **Germany**

中国人民银行 VK 66513596 貳角 2 ER JIAO
▲ **People's Republic of China**

▲ **Japan**

▲ **Mexico**

▲ **Malawi**

▲ **Canada**

Activity 14: Match

1. *Part a.* Working together as a class, tell what you see on each coin pictured here. Write any unfamiliar words on the board. Then have students locate each country on a world map.

2. Give pairs of students a copy of AM 3/7. Together record information about the German coin, using checkmarks as in the chart on this page. Then have pairs record information about the other coins on the page. Have pairs get together in groups to compare charts.

3. Ask students to bring in coins from other countries and add information to the chart. (Students will look at U.S. coins in the next activity, so don't study them yet.)

4. Encourage more proficient learners to tell the class about the currency in their native countries.

(Continued on page 56.)

Activity 14: Match *(continued)*

5. *Part b.* Have students look at the pictures of U.S. coins or better yet give groups of students actual coins. Ask them to study the faces on the coins and tell how they are similar and different. Ask: *Which man has a beard? Which man has long hair? Which man has a modern haircut?* Use gestures and drawings to clarify unfamiliar words.

6. Read aloud the questions on page 56 while students look at the coins. Ask if anyone wants to make a guess, using the model in the Language Focus box on page 56.

7. Direct students' attention to the first portrait on page 56. Ask them to find this person's name. Then ask: *Who was George Washington?* Give students time to look over the information about Washington. Then list their ideas on the board. Repeat with the other pictures on pages 56 and 57.

8. Have students use the portraits to guess the person on each coin, using the model in the Language Focus box on page 56. Then have pairs combine into groups of four to compare answers. Find out how they made their guesses. What information in the portraits helped them to guess?

9. Read aloud the information about each president. Then have volunteers tell something they learned about each president.

(Continued on page 57.)

b. Pairwork. Use the information on these pages to answer the questions below.

1. Who is on a penny?

2. Who is on a nickel?

3. Who is on a dime?

4. Who is on a quarter?

5. Who is on a half-dollar?

Language Focus

- I think it's Abraham Lincoln.
- I think Abraham Lincoln is on the penny.

George Washington
1732–1799
President 1789–1797

George Washington was commander in chief of the Continental Army during the American Revolutionary War (1775–1783). He later became the first president of the United States.

Thomas Jefferson
1743–1826
President 1801–1809

Thomas Jefferson was the third president of the United States. He was also an architect, inventor, lawyer, and writer. He wrote the first draft of the Declaration of Independence.

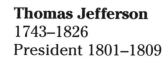

Abraham Lincoln
1809–1865
President 1861–1865

Abraham Lincoln was the sixteenth president of the United States.
He was president during the American Civil War.

Franklin D. Roosevelt
1882–1945
President 1933–1945

Franklin Roosevelt was the thirty-second president of the United States. He was president during the second World War.

John F. Kennedy
1917–1963
President 1961–1963

John Kennedy was the thirty-fifth president of the United States.

c. Complete a chart like this. Add information about coins from other countries.

Coin	Country	Person on coin
penny	USA	Abraham Lincoln
nickel	USA	
dime	USA	
quarter	USA	
half-dollar	USA	

Language Focus

A: Who's on a Canadian quarter?
B: Queen Elizabeth II.

10. *Part c.* Give each student a copy of AM 3/8. Ask about the people on U.S. coins, using the model in the Language Focus box on page 57. For example, *Who's on a U.S. penny?* Students can add their answer to the chart. For homework, have students collect information about coins from their native country and add it to the chart. At your next class, have them share information and make a class chart about coins from different countries.

Activity Menu

Read the activities to the class and answer any questions. Then have students individually or in small groups select a project for a class or homework assignment. Projects can be shared with the class and/or displayed in the classroom.

Note that answers for Activity 6, (page 43) are at the bottom of page 59.

Activity Menu

Choose one of the following activities to do.

1. Spending Money
Keep a list of your purchases for a week. List everything you buy. Write the price. At the end of a week, find the total.

Day of Week	Purchase	Cost
Monday	lunch notebook	

2. Make a Poster
Make a poster showing the money in your native country. Draw and label the money. Share your poster with the class.

3. Make a Menu
Make a menu with your favorite foods. List the foods and give them a price. Let your classmates practice ordering food from your menu.

4. Plan a Saturday Outing
Plan something special to do on Saturday. Look in the newspaper for ideas. Answer these questions:
- Where will you go?
- How much will it cost?
- How will you get there and back?
- How much will transportation cost?

Report your plan to the class.

5. Dollar Shopping
Visit a store and look for things that cost less than $1.00. How many things can you find? List them. Report what you learned to the class.

6. Collect Money Expressions

Collect expressions about money from several languages and cultures. Report on their meaning.

Example:

"You look like a million bucks." (You look wonderful.)
"A penny for your thoughts." (What are you thinking about?)

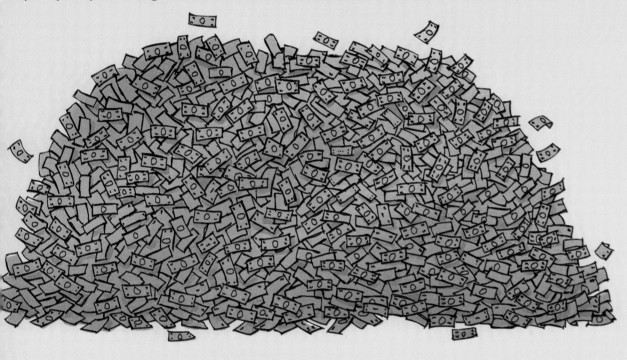

Answers for Activity 6 (page 43)

microscope – $750.00	dictionary – $12.95	notebook – $1.19
computer – $1500.00	eraser – .49	globe – $35.99

Sweater ▽

Woman's Suit ▽

Man's Suit

Socks ▽

Sneakers

Sweatshirt ▽

Shirt ▽

Tie ▽

Baseball cap ▽

Skirt ▲

▲ Sweatpants

Choosing Clothes

◀ **Dress**

Gym shorts

▼ **Blue jeans**

▼ **Coat**

T-shirt

| 1. | Identify |

Classwork. Listen and identify the clothes.

Jacket

Boots

Student text pages 60–61

Activity 1: Identify

1. Point to each article of clothing on pages 60 and 61 and name it. Name articles of clothing in random order and have students point to the pictures in their book. Play the tape and let students listen and point to the clothing.

2. Ask yes/no questions about the clothes on pages 60–61: *Do you like the sweatshirt? Do you like the dress?*

3. For additional practice, students can play a clothing lotto game. Give each student a copy of AM 4/1 or have them draw and number a lotto card with four rows of four inch-and-a-half squares. (The top row is numbered 1, 2, 3, 4; the next row 5, 6, 7, 8; etc.)

4. Give each student a copy of AM 4/2 and have them cut out the pictures of clothing. At the same time, you can prepare your own lotto card to use as a script for the game. To do this, cut out the pictures on your copy of AM 4/2 and tape one article of clothing in each square of the lotto card, in random order. Tell students to listen and follow your instructions. Without showing your lotto card, give instructions for making one like it, naming the articles of clothing and the square ("box") numbers where each is to go. For example, say, *Put a pair of shoes in Box 5. Put a shirt in Box 11.* Continue until students have placed an article of clothing in each square of their card. Show your lotto card and let students compare. Then students can take turns being the game host, using different arrangements of the clothing articles.

Activity 2: Describe

1. Describe the clothing of the people on pages 62-63. For example, *Anna's wearing a T-shirt and blue jeans.* As students listen, they can point to each article of clothing. Then have students take turns describing each person's clothing.

2. Read aloud the names of the colors and patterns in the circle chart and let students repeat after you. Model the question and answer in the Language Focus box. Then let students take turns asking and answering questions about the people on pages 62–63.

3. Write these questions on the board: *Do you like Marissa's skirt? Do you like Andy's suit?* Read the questions aloud and let volunteers answer. Encourage students to ask other questions, using the model on the board.

4. Write this question on the board: *What color is Tony's baseball cap?* Let a volunteer answer and then form a new question, using the model on the board.

5. Play a "stand up" game incorporating color words and names of clothing. For example, say: *Stand up if you are wearing blue jeans. Stand up if you are wearing a white shirt.*

2. Describe

Classwork. What are these people wearing?

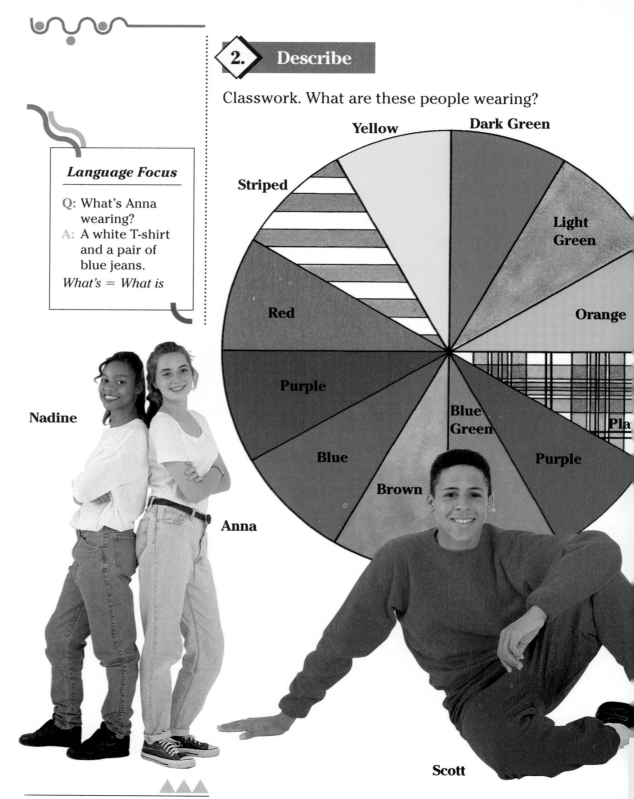

Language Focus

Q: What's Anna wearing?
A: A white T-shirt and a pair of blue jeans.
What's = What is

Marissa

Andy

Karen

Tony

Student text pages 64–65

Activity 3: Listen

1. Together identify the clothing on pages 64 and 65. You might, for example, have students take turns listing on the board an item of clothing pictured here.

2. In this activity, students will first hear a male student telling about his friends. The speaker and his friends are pictured on page 64. Students should listen and by process of elimination, identify the speaker's clothing. Play the tape or read the script. Encourage students to point to each person being described. Let students listen again and then describe the speaker's clothing. (Answer: He's wearing shorts and a red sweatshirt.)

3. In the second part of this activity, students will hear a female student telling about her friends. These people are pictured on page 65. Play the tape or read the script. Encourage students to point to each person being described. Let students listen again and then describe the speaker's clothing. (Answer: She's wearing a dress.)

4. Extend the activity by listing on the board these names: *Martin, Fernando, Greg, Tony, Norio, Debora, Anna, Jane, Maria, Taka.* See if students can match any of these names with the pictures. Ask: *What is Martin wearing? What is Greg wearing?* List any answers on the board. Ask students to copy the names onto a piece of paper. Then play the tapescript again and let them take notes. Students can check their answers by asking and answering questions. For example, *What's Martin wearing? A suit and tie.* Finally ask, *Who is Norio?* Point to him. *Who is Taka?* Point to her.

5. Have volunteers bring to class photographs of friends or family members. Let them tell the class about the people in the photographs.

3. Listen

Classwork. Listen to the tape and study the pictures.

What am I wearing?

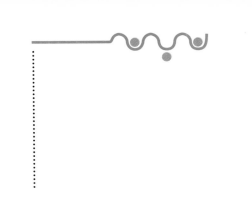

Activity 4: Write

1. *Part a.* Describe your clothes in writing on the board. Hand out identical pieces of paper and have students write about their clothing, but not put their names on their paper.

2. *Part b.* Collect the papers, mix them up, and redistribute them. Have students read the description they have received aloud. Let the class identify the writer.

Activity 5: Interview

1. *Part a.* While students look at the pictures on page 66, write these sentences on the board: *I like the blue pants a lot. The brown pants are okay. I don't like the plaid pants at all.* Read the sentences aloud, using tone of voice and facial expressions to help convey meaning.

2. Have students turn back to pages 64–65. Model the sentences in the Language Focus box on page 67 by telling about your clothing likes and dislikes, e.g., *I like the red sweater a lot. I don't like the dress at all.* Let students tell about their likes and dislikes.

3. On the board write, *I like it a lot. I like it okay. I don't like it at all.* Have students turn to page 1 and answer these questions: *Do you like the green sweater? Do you like the yellow sweater?* Let students answer choosing from the sentences on the board.

4. On the board write, *I like them a lot. I like them okay. I don't like them at all.* Then have students turn to pages 62–63 and answer these questions: *Do you like Karen's shoes? Do you like Tony's shoes?* Let students answer, choosing from the sentences on the board.

5. Model Activity #5 with a student. Ask your partner the questions on page 67 and show how to record the answers on a chart. Give each student a copy of AM 4/3 and have them form pairs to ask questions and complete the chart. Tell them to hold on to their charts.

(Continued on page 67.)

---

4. Write

a. On your own. Describe your clothing.

What are you wearing?

I am wearing jeans, a green sweater, and sneakers.

b. Read a classmate's description aloud. Ask your classmates to guess the person.

5. Interview

a. Pairwork. Look at the chart on page 67. Interview a partner. Record your partner's answers in a chart.

Q: Do you like the *red sweater*?
A: Yes, I like it a lot. (It's okay. No, I don't like it at all.)

Q: Do you like the *brown pants*?
A: Yes, I like them a lot. (They're okay. No, I don't like them at all.)

Do you like the . . . ?	a lot +++	okay +	not at all −
red sweater			
sweatshirt			
T-shirt			
_____			

b. Classwork. Listen and write the price for each article of clothing.

Article of clothing	Price
red sweater	_____
sweatshirt	_____
_____	_____

c. On your own. Buy an outfit for your partner. Choose clothes your partner likes from the pictures on pages 68–69. Follow the steps below to write a store receipt.

1. List each article of clothing.
2. Write the price for each article of clothing.
3. Add the prices to find the subtotal.
4. To find the tax, multiply the subtotal by .085.
5. To find the total, add the subtotal and the tax.

Language Focus

- I like the red sweater a lot.
  I like **it** a lot.
- I like the brown pants a lot.
  I like **them** a lot.

---

6. *Part b.* Together, guess the price of each article of clothing on page 66. Let students write the amounts on the board; clarify any problems with the position of the dollar sign and the use of the decimal point.

7. Tell students they will hear ten short conversations. They should listen and write the price of each item. Show them where to write their answers on AM 4/3. Play the tape. (Answers: red sweater, $18.00; sweatshirt, $12.00; T-shirt, $9.00; plaid pants, $24.00; brown pants, $32.00; blue jeans, $28.00; brown shoes, $25.00; white sneakers, $45.00; red shoes, $18.00; black shoes, $36.00.)

8. *Part c.* Give each student a copy of AM 4/4 or have them copy the store receipt on page 68 without the examples. Ask them to put their names on the reverse side of the paper.

9. Model the activity. Look at one student's chart from Part a. Choose an outfit from the articles of clothing that the person likes. Draw a receipt on the board and list these articles. Write the prices from Part b and find a subtotal. Calculate the tax (8.5%) and find the total. Do your calculations aloud so students hear your step-by-step problem solving. Have the class choose an outfit for you and fill out a receipt on the board.

10. Put students in pairs. Have each choose an outfit for his or her partner and fill out the store receipt. Circulate and answer any questions.

11. Collect the receipts, mix them up, and post them on a wall. Have students look them over and choose an outfit they like. They should check the math on the receipt, then describe the outfit to the class and tell what it costs. Then have them check the name on the reverse side. Is it their partner's?

(Continued on page 68.)

Activity 5: Interview (continued)

12. *Part d.* Write this sentence on the board: I spent _____. Have students tell how much money they spent and then together answer the questions.

13. For additional practice, try this TPR activity. Label one section of the board *store* and another section *closet*. Cut out pictures of clothing from magazines and tape them to the board in the store section. Have the class decide on prices and write them on the board.

14. Demonstrate Script A below. Then read the script aloud and let students take turns following the instructions. If possible, bring in Monopoly or play money for students to use. When students have mastered Script A, introduce Script B.

Script A	Script B
Go to the store.	Go to your closet.
Find the ___.	Try your new ___ on.
Try it on. Look in the mirror.	Look in the mirror.
Smile. You like it.	Frown. You don't like it.
Give the money to the clerk.	Take it back to the store.
Get a receipt.	Bring your receipt.
Take your clothing home.	Get your money back.
Hang it in your closet.	

Activity 6: Solve

1. Introduce this activity by asking about the prices of the clothing on page 68. For example, *How much do the brown shoes cost?* Tell students that these clothes are now on sale for 50% off. To find the sale price of the brown shoes, follow the steps in the box. Do the simple math on the board explaining the steps as you go along, so that students hear the language of math. Tell students that the clothes on page 69 are on sale for 20% off. Follow the steps in the box to find the sale price of the black shoes.

2. Put students in groups to find the sale price of each item. Have them write the prices on another sheet of paper.

(Continued on page 69.)

 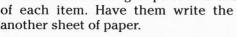

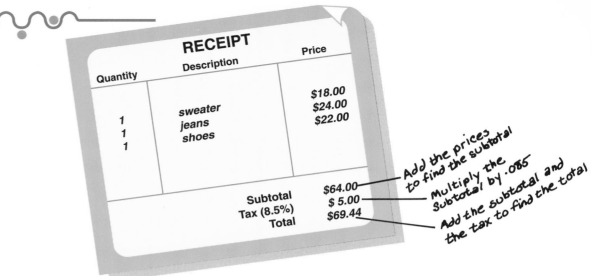

RECEIPT

Quantity	Description	Price
1	sweater	$18.00
1	jeans	$24.00
1	shoes	$22.00
	Subtotal	$64.00
	Tax (8.5%)	$ 5.00
	Total	$69.44

Add the prices to find the subtotal

Multiply the Subtotal by .085

Add the subtotal and the tax to find the total

d. Classwork. Compare receipts. Who spent the most money? Who spent the least money? Who spent the same amount of money?

6. ◆ **Solve**

Groupwork. How much do these clothes cost? Figure out the prices. Then answer the questions below.

SALE Take 50% off

Take 50% off

> 1. Multiply the price by .50.
> 2. Subtract the result from the price.
> Example:
> $38.00 × .50 = $19.00
> $38.00 − $19.00 = $19.00

Sale Price

brown shoes *$19.00*

black pants _____

leather jacket _____

white sweatshirt _____

SALE
Take 20% off

3. Let the groups compare answers. (Answers: brown shoes, $19.00; black pants, $23.00; black leather jacket, $79.00; white sweatshirt, $11.00; light brown pants, $25.60; denim jacket, $72.00; blue sweatshirt, $12.00)

4. Have groups answer the questions, using their list of sale prices. (Answers: a. brown shoes; b. black pants; c. leather jacket; d. blue sweatshirt)

5. For a follow-up activity, students can look through the newspaper to find examples of store sales that give the amount of discount (for example, all items 50% off). Have them draw or find a picture of something that could be for sale in this store and write a price tag with the original price. Attach this to the ad. Have pairs exchange papers and figure out the sale price. Have them describe the ad to the class and report their results. For example, *This chair costs $60. It's on sale for 30% off. On sale it costs $42.00.*

Take 20% off

> 1. Multiply the price by .20.
> 2. Subtract the result from the price.
>
> Example:
> $26.00 × .20 = $5.20
> $26.00 − $5.20 = $20.80

Sale Price

black shoes $20.80

light brown pants _____

denim jacket _____

blue sweatshirt _____

a. Which pair of shoes is cheaper? _the brown shoes_

b. Which pair of pants is cheaper? _____

c. Which jacket is more expensive? _____

d. Which sweatshirt is more expensive? _____

Activity 7: Compare

1. *Part a.* Introduce the pictures by asking about students' likes and dislikes. For example, Q: *Do you like the white dress?* A: *Yes, I like it a lot.*

2. Write these adjectives on the board: *pretty, fancy, baggy, warm, comfortable, long, nice.* Have students turn back to pages 62–63 and listen while you tell about the clothing, using the words on the board. For example, *I think Marissa's skirt is pretty. Anna's shoes are comfortable.* Encourage volunteers to give their opinions.

3. Write the comparative form of the adjectives on the board: *prettier, fancier, baggier, more comfortable, longer, nicer.* Then ask questions about the clothing on pages 62 and 63. For example, *Which skirt is longer? Which pants are baggier? Which shoes are more comfortable?*

4. Now have students look at the clothing on pages 70 and 71. Copy on the board the chart on page 70. Include only the first two questions. Model this activity by writing your opinion about the first question in the appropriate column of the chart. For example, *the blue dress.* Then ask one student: *Which dress is prettier?* Write this student's answer in the appropriate column. Repeat with the second question.

5. Give each student a copy of AM 4/5. Put students in pairs to add their opinions and their partner's opinions to the chart. After completing the chart, students can take turns reporting their answers. For example, *We both think the white dress is prettier. My partner thinks the blue dress is prettier but I think the white dress is prettier.*

(Continued on page 71.)

7. Compare

a. Pairwork. Answer these questions. Record your answers in a chart.

	My Opinion	My Partner's Opinion
1. Which dress is prettier?		
2. Which dress is fancier?		
3. Which pants are baggier?		
4. Which jacket is warmer?		
5. Which women's shoes are more comfortable?		
6. Which skirt is longer?		
7. Which sneakers are nicer?		

b. Pairwork. Practice the dialogue below.

A: Which ___*skirt*___ do you like better?

B: The ___*plaid skirt*___ .

A: Why?

B: Because ___*it's prettier*___ .

c. Pairwork. Tell the class about your partner.

Example: *My partner likes the plaid skirt better.*

Language Focus

- The white dress is prettier.
- The white athletic shoes are more comfortable.

warm	→ warmer
long	→ longer
nice	→ nicer
pretty	→ prettier
fancy	→ fancier
baggy	→ baggier
comfortable	↳ more comfortable

▲▲▲

Activity 7: Compare *(continued)*

Part b. Model the dialogue with a student. Then have pairs practice the dialogue, substituting different types of clothing (shoes, dress, jacket, pants, skirt). Circulate during the activity to listen to their conversations.

Part c. Have students report one of their partner's opinions.

For follow up, have students study the comparative forms of adjectives in the Language Focus box on page 71. Work together to infer the rules for comparative forms of adjectives.

- For most one-syllable adjectives, add -er. (warmer, longer)

- For two-syllable words that end in -y, change the -y to -i and add -er. (prettier, baggier)

- For words with three or more syllables, use more. (more comfortable)

Together make a chart of adjectives with their comparative forms to keep on a classroom wall. Encourage students to add to the chart as they encounter new words.

Activity 8: Match

1. Together identify the clothing on this page. Help students with unfamiliar words related to the pictures and write them on the board. Have students compare the hats shown here. For example, *Which hat is warmer?*

2. Read the instruction line and the captions aloud. Put students in groups and have each group number a piece of paper from 1 to 6. They should then write the appropriate captions next to each number. While they may not understand all of the words, they should have enough information to match the captions and pictures.

3. Have groups compare answers.

4. Encourage students to think of other clothing that protects the body. Make a class chart of protective clothing and have students add to it as they think of new ideas.

1

8. Match

Groupwork. These clothes have a special purpose. They protect the body. Match the pictures and the captions.

2

Surgeons wear face masks to protect themselves from germs.

People wear seat belts to protect their bodies if they have a car accident.

People wear sunglasses to protect their eyes from the sun.

Football players wear helmets to protect their heads.

In cold weather, people wear hats to stay warm.

People wear hats with visors to protect their heads and eyes from the sun.

5

3

4

6

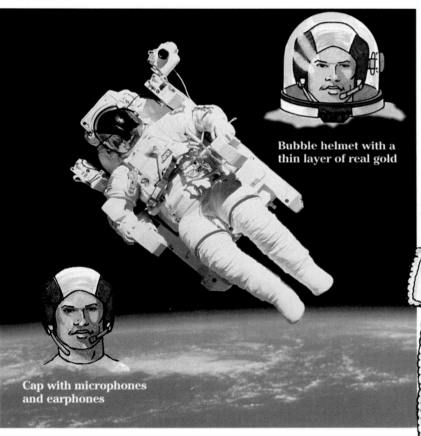

9. Guess

a. Groupwork. What's the purpose of this special clothing? Answer the questions below.

Astronauts wear special clothes when they walk in space.

Bubble helmet with a thin layer of real gold

Cap with microphones and earphones

Language Focus

Q: Why do astronauts wear water-cooled underwear?
A: To stay cool.

Special water-cooled underwear

Space suit with a computer inside

1. Why do astronauts wear water-cooled underwear?

2. Why do they wear space suits? Why do the space suits have a computer inside?

3. Why do they wear caps with microphones and earphones?

4. Why do they wear bubble helmets? Why do the helmets have a thin layer of gold?

b. Compare your ideas with the answers on page 74.

Activity 9: Guess

1. Together identify the space clothing shown in the labeled pictures.

2. Read aloud the *why* question in the Language Focus box. Then together think of other questions about the pictures. For example, *Why do astronauts wear a cap with microphones?*

3. Put students in groups to guess answers to the questions on page 73.

Part b. Let groups compare answers and then check against the answers on page 74.

(Continued on page 74.)

Activity 9: Guess *(continued)*

Be ready to discuss these answers to the four questions at the end of Part a on page 73.

Activity 10: Share Ideas

1. *Part a.* Together describe the clothing on page 75. List any new words on the board.

2. Ask students to look at the chart on page 74. Clarify the three categories by listing examples of clothing that people wear to protect the body, to be in style, and because it's a custom. Point out that styles change while customs stay the same.

3. Give each student a copy of AM 4/6 or have them copy the chart on this page. Read aloud the dialogues in the Language Focus box and have students add the answers to their chart.

4. Give students time to answer the remaining questions in the chart. Then let volunteers take turns asking and answering the questions.

5. Put students in groups to add more questions to the chart. For example, *Why do motorcyclists wear helmets?* Have them read their questions aloud and let their classmates answer.

6. Extend this activity by asking students to collect pictures of interesting clothing. Have them write a question to accompany each picture and then post the pictures and questions on a classroom wall for the rest of the class to study.

(Continued on page 76.)

(Answers)
1. They wear water-cooled underwear to keep cool.
2. They wear space suits to protect their bodies. The space suits provide the right amount of air pressure for their bodies. The computer tells them if the suit is working properly.
3. They wear caps with microphones and earphones to communicate, or talk to each other.
4. The bubble helmets fill with air. This allows the astronauts to breathe. The helmets have a thin layer of gold to protect the astronauts' eyes from the sun.

10. ◆ Share Ideas

a. Classwork. Why do you think people wear these clothes? Record your ideas in a chart like this.

	to protect the body	to be in style	because it's a custom
Why do students in the United States wear black robes at graduation?			✓
Why do some people wear neckties?			
Why do some women wear high-heeled shoes?			
Why do some people in the desert wear loose robes?			
Why do workers on a ranch wear boots?			
In some countries, brides wear white dresses. In some countries, they wear red dresses. Why?			

▲▲▲

Language Focus

Q: Why do students in the United States wear black robes at graduation?

A: Because it's a custom.

Q: Why do some women wear high-heeled shoes?

A: To be in style.

Activity 10: Share Ideas *(continued)*

Part b. Have groups of students copy the chart on page 76. Work together as a class to add several ideas to the chart. Then let groups work on their own to add more ideas to their chart. Students *can* then use their chart to ask their classmates *why* questions. For example, *Why do people in Japan sometimes wear kimonos?*

Activity 11: Plan

1. *Parts a, b, and c.* Bring to class a picture of a vacation spot. Choose a picture that shows people doing something. Display the picture and tell students that they can visit this place for a week. Together make a cluster diagram showing what you are going to do there.

2. Draw a simple picture of a suitcase on the board and ask: *What are you going to take in your suitcase?* Together brainstorm ideas and list them on the board.

3. Together study the pictures on this page. Ask: *What are the people doing? Where are they? What are they wearing?* Together find each of these places on a U.S. map. If possible, bring in reference books or travel books to provide more information about each of these places.

4. Put students in groups to choose one of these places to visit for a week. They should keep their choice a secret from the other groups. Work with individual groups to help them make a cluster diagram showing what they plan to do in their place of choice. Encourage them to look back at Unit 2 for ideas. Then have groups fill their suitcase, listing the items they will take.

(Continued on page 77.)

b. Groupwork. Add your ideas to a chart like this.

What do people wear to protect their bodies?	What do people wear to be in style?	What do people wear because it's a custom?
gloves		kimonos (Japan)

11. **Plan**

a. Groupwork. Take a trip. Choose one of these places to visit for a week.

A ranch in Texas

The island of Hawaii

The mountains in Maine

b. What are you going to do there? Brainstorm a set of ideas.

 *ride bikes*   *swim*

things to do

Language Focus

- We're going to swim.
- We're going to ride bikes.

c. Choose ten articles of clothing to take in your suitcase.
Example: *I'm going to take a jacket.*

d. Exchange lists with another group. Which place are they going to visit? Make a guess.

 12. Write

a. On your own. Follow the steps below.

1. Find or draw a picture of an interesting outfit.
2. Label all the parts.
3. Where are you going to wear this outfit? Write your answer on a card like this.

> *I'm going to wear this outfit to*
> _____ .

b. Classwork. Mix up everyone's cards and pictures. Then try to match them.

13. Shared Reading

a. Classwork. Study the shoes in the picture on the next page. Choose words to describe the shoes.

These words are opposites.

cheap	↔	expensive
soft	↔	stiff
clean	↔	dirty
comfortable	↔	uncomfortable
old	↔	new

Language Focus

- I'm going to wear this outfit to go on a picnic.
- I'm going to wear this outfit to play basketball.

Language Focus

- I think they are expensive.
- They look expensive.

Activity 11: Plan *(continued)*

5. *Part d.* Ask groups to exchange lists and guess where the other group is going.

6. If the groups chose different destinations, tell them there is a problem. The suitcases got mixed up at the airport. Give them their new suitcases i.e., give them another group's suitcase—one for a different climate. Have them consider what problems they will have, given the mixup.

Activity 12: Write

1. *Parts a and b.* To model the activity, cut out a picture of someone wearing an outfit that you like. Tape the picture to a piece of paper and label each piece of clothing. On another piece of paper, tell where you are going to wear this clothing. For example, *I am going to wear this outfit at home.* Show your work to the class. Then read the examples in the Language Focus box for other ideas.

2. Let students cut out or draw interesting outfits. Help them to label the clothing. On another piece of paper, they should complete this sentence: *I'm going to wear this outfit* _____ .

3. Collect the labeled pictures and written statements. Post them on a wall and have students match them.

Activity 13: Shared Reading

1. *Part a.* Have students look at the pair of shoes on page 78. Together think of words to describe the shoes and list them on the board. Read the list of antonyms ("opposites") on page 77 and have students add more words to the list on the board. Use the model in the Language Focus box to describe the shoes.

(Continued on page 78.)

Activity 13: Shared Reading *(continued)*

2. *Part b.* Play the tape or read the poem aloud. Divide the class into two groups and have groups take turns reading a line. Have partners take turns reading a line to each other.

3. Ask students to find words in the poem that describe the shoes. Have them take turns coming to the board to list these words.

4. Read aloud the definition of an ode. Then have volunteers tell why this poet likes his shoes. Write the reasons on the board as they are given and discuss them with the class.

> ### What's an Ode?
>
> An ode is a poem that praises something. It tells why the poet likes something.

b. Classwork. Read this poem aloud with your classmates.

Ode to My Shoes

My shoes from America,
they are very expensive and soft.
They help me to walk.
When I go somewhere,
they go with me, too.
They come to school with me.
When I go back home,
my shoes stay under my bed.
Sometimes they look very happy.
When they are torn,
they look like they are smiling.
When they are dirty,
they look very sleepy.
I like my shoes.

—*Harjit Singh (former student, Newcomer High School)*

14. Write

a. On your own. What's your favorite clothing?

My favorite clothing is ___a pair of blue sweatpants___ .

b. List words to describe your favorite clothing.
   ___blue, old, holey, comfortable___

c. Quickwrite about your favorite clothing. Try to write without stopping for three minutes. Here are some questions you might think about as you write:

1. What does this clothing look like?
2. Where do you like to wear this clothing?
3. How do you feel when you wear this clothing?

Example:

My favorite clothing is a pair of blue sweatpants. They are very old and they have lots of holes. But they are very comfortable. I feel energetic when I wear them. At night I hang them over a chair. Then they look tired. I only wear them at home because they are so old. My mother wants to throw them out but I won't let her....

c. Use the ideas in your quickwriting to write an ode to your favorite clothing.

Activity 14: Write

1. *Part a.* Model the activity by identifying your favorite article of clothing. Write a sentence about it on the board. For example, *My favorite clothing is a purple sweatshirt.* Let volunteers identify their favorite clothing.

2. *Part b.* List words to describe your favorite clothing. For example, *soft, warm, faded, light.* If possible, bring in this article of clothing for the class to see. Have students list words to describe their favorite clothing.

3. *Part c.* Introduce quickwriting by modeling it for the class. Write rapidly on the board about your favorite clothing. For several minutes, try to write without stopping. If you get stuck simply repeat words or write: *I don't know what to write.* Leave your quickwriting on the board. Then have students quickwrite for three minutes about their favorite article of clothing.

4. *Part d.* Using ideas from your quickwriting, write a simple ode to your favorite article of clothing. Let students see how you change ideas, cross things out, and revise your writing.

5. Give students time to use ideas from their own quickwriting to write their odes to their favorite clothing.

Activity Menu

Read the activities to the class and answer any questions. Then have students individually or in small groups select a project to do in class or as a homework assignment. Projects can later be shared with the class and/or displayed in the classroom.

Activity Menu

Choose one of the following activities to do.

1. School Dress Code
The school dress code tells what you can and can't wear at school. What is the dress code at your school? Copy and illustrate the rules, and post them in your classroom.

2. Spend $100 on Clothes
Imagine that you have $100 to spend on new clothes. Look through a catalog of clothing, and make your choices. Fill out an order form, and show it to your classmates. Make sure you don't spend more than $100.

3. Clothing Around the World
Study pictures of people in a different country. Tell your classmates about the clothing in this country.

4. Clothing Advice
What do people in your native country wear at this time of year? Tell your classmates what clothes to take on a trip to your native country.

5. Collect Pictures
Collect pictures of people in different professions. Group the people by profession. Describe their clothing, and tell your classmates what people wear to work in different professions.

6. Clothing for Special Occasions
Write about a ceremony in which people wear special clothing. Describe the clothing and the occasion. Share your writing with your classmates.

7. Taking Care of Clothes

Read the labels on several items of clothing. Find out from what kinds of fabric they are made. Read the cleaning or washing instructions. Write the information in a chart. Show your chart to the class.

Kind of fabric	Instructions
100% Acrylic	Machine wash cold Tumble dry low Do not bleach

8. Make a Pie Graph

Choose an article of clothing made from different kinds of fabrics. Make a pie graph showing the percentage of each fabric.

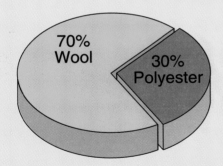

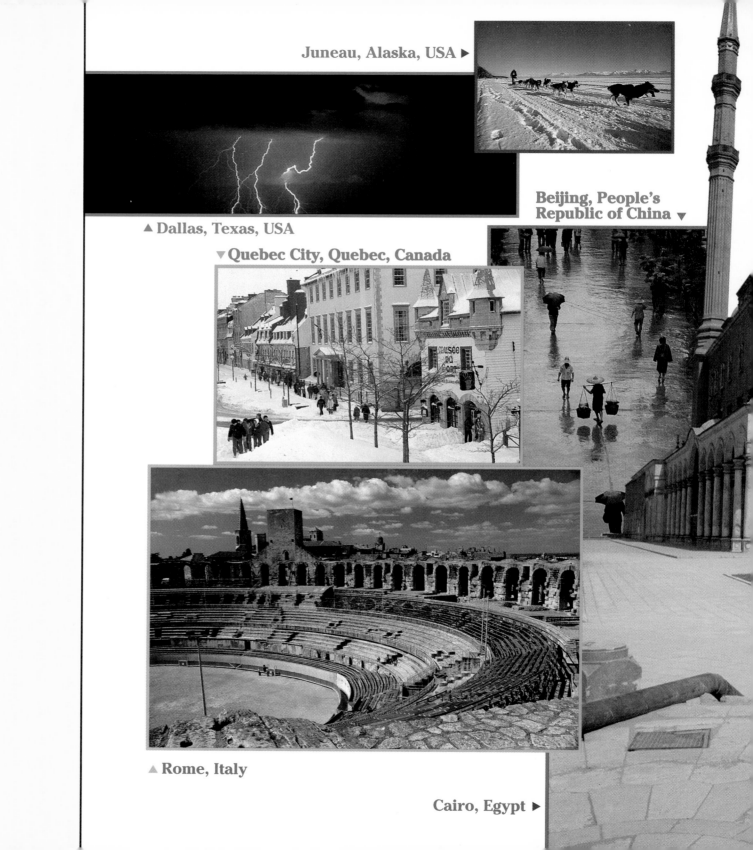

Juneau, Alaska, USA ▶

▲ Dallas, Texas, USA

Beijing, People's
Republic of China ▼

▼ Quebec City, Quebec, Canada

▲ Rome, Italy

Cairo, Egypt ▶

Checking the Weather

▲ San Juan, Puerto Rico

▲ Montreal, Quebec, Canada

1. **Listen**

Classwork. Listen and point to the cities.

Student text pages 82–83

Activity 1: Listen

1. Together study the pictures taken in different parts of the world. Ask: *What do you see in the picture of Juneau?* Let volunteers answer while you help with unfamiliar words. Repeat with the other pictures. Then have students locate each place on a world map.

2. Tell students they will hear a description of the weather in each of these cities. They should listen and point to the cities. Play the tape or read the script twice.

3. Review yes/no questions: *Is it raining in Beijing? Is it snowing in Quebec City?* Review short answer questions: *Is it sunny or cloudy in Cairo?* Then have volunteers take turns telling about the weather in each city.

4. There may be some confusion about the use of present continuous verbs (it is raining / it is snowing) and the verb *to be* with adjectives (it is cloudy / it is sunny). Put these four examples on the board in two columns. Elicit other weather words and put them in the appropriate columns.

Activity 2: Identify

1. *Part a.* Have students find each of these cities on a map of North America. Review clothing vocabulary by asking students to describe people's clothing in the pictures.

2. Read the sentences in the Language Focus box on page 85 aloud. Point to a picture in the book and have students describe the weather, using a sentence from the Language Focus box.

3. Have students number a paper from 1 - 6. Tell them to listen and write the name of the city next to the correct number on their paper. Play the tape or read the script. Let students listen again to check their answers.

4. Students can compare answers by describing the weather in each city. For example, *It's snowing in Portland.*

5. Bring in today's newspaper and have students look at the photographs in different places and describe the weather. Encourage them to look at the clothing people are wearing and to make inferences.

(Continued on page 85.)

2. Identify

a. Classwork. Listen and identify these cities.

Boston, Massachusetts, USA
Chicago, Illinois, USA
Toronto, Quebec, Canada

Mexico City, Mexico
Portland, Maine, USA
Vancouver, British Columbia, Canada

6. *Part b.* On another piece of paper, students should describe today's weather. Then let students compare descriptions.

7. For follow-up, have students keep a chart of the weather, adding a short description each day.

Language Focus

It's raining in Boston.

It's raining.	It's sunny.
It's snowing.	It's cloudy.
It's storming.	It's windy.
	It's cold.
	It's cool.
	It's warm.
	It's hot.

---

b. On your own. Write about the weather in your area today.

Activity 3: Read Symbols

1. *Part a.* Have students point to the cities on the weather map as you read the names.

2. Make two columns on the board with the headings *Today* and *Tomorrow.* In each column, add the day of the week, date, and weather information for your area.

Today	Tomorrow
Tuesday	Wednesday
November 18	November 19
It's sunny.	It's going to be sunny.

3. Go over the weather symbols in the map key on this page. Describe tomorrow's weather in several cities while students listen and find the cities. For example, *It's going to snow in New York.* Then let volunteers tell about tomorrow's weather in different cities. Point out that in speaking people often say *it's gonna,* but it's always written *it's going to.*

4. Have students choose a place on the map and tell about the weather. When they report to the class, ask them to repeat the previous student's statement. For example, Student 1 says: *It's going to be cloudy in Dallas.* Student 2 says: *It's going to be cloudy in Dallas and it's going to rain in Seattle.*

5. For follow-up, bring in the weather forecast from your newspaper for students to read. Bring in yesterday's forecast to see if it was correct.

Part b. Write this example on the board: *It's going to be sunny in Miami and El Paso.* Read the sentence aloud and then erase the names of the cities and have students add other names. Write *Seattle* and *Vancouver* on the board and have students write a sentence. Then have pairs work together to write sentences describing the weather in two cities.

3. Read Symbols

a. Pairwork. Choose a place on the weather map. Describe tomorrow's weather.

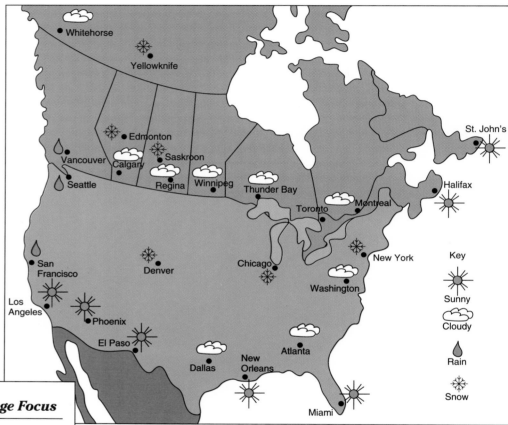

Language Focus

- It's going to be sunny in Miami tomorrow.
- It's going to be cloudy in Calgary tomorrow.
- It's going to rain in Seattle.
- It's going to snow in Yellowknife.

b. Pairwork. Find two places with the same weather symbols. Describe the weather.

Example: *It's going to be sunny in Miami and El Paso.*

4. Listen

a. Classwork. What are they going to do tomorrow?
   Listen and complete a chart.

	Dialogue #1	Dialogue #2
What's the weather going to be like?	_____	_____
What are they going to do tomorrow?	_____	_____

b. Pairwork. Read a weather forecast for your area.
   Then practice this dialogue.

A: What do you want to do tomorrow?

B: I don't know. I think it's going to _be sunny_ .

A: Then let's _do something outdoors_ .

B: Okay.

c. On your own. Answer these questions.

1. What are you going to do tomorrow if it rains?
   If it rains tomorrow, I am going to _____ .

2. What are you going to do tomorrow if it's sunny?
   If it's sunny tomorrow, I _____ .

Activity 4: Listen

1. *Part a.* Read aloud the questions in the chart. Tell students they will hear two dialogues. They should listen for answers to the questions and take notes on another piece of paper. Play the tape or read the script. Let students listen again to check their answers. (Answers: 1. It's going to rain. They're going to go to a movie. 2. It's going to be sunny. They're going to do something outdoors.)

2. *Part b.* Read the sample dialogue aloud with a student. Choose a city on the weather map on page 86 and model the dialogue again.

3. Copy on the board the weather forecast for your area. Let pairs practice the dialogue, using the information in the weather forecast. Have volunteers perform for the class.

4. Extend the activity by having students pretend they are in one of the cities on the weather map on page 86. Let them practice the dialogue, using the weather forecast for this city.

5. *Part c.* Let students work on their own to complete these sentences. Have them write their sentences on another piece of paper. Post the papers on a wall so that students can read each other's ideas. Have students look for similar answers and group the papers.

Activity 5: Describe

1. Bring in yesterday's newspaper. You or the students can cut out pictures of outdoor scenes and identify the location of each picture. Introduce the past form of the verb *to be* by describing the weather in each picture. For example, *Yesterday it was sunny in Miami.* Students can listen and then take turns telling about yesterday's weather in these locations.

2. Copy on the board the chart on page 88, substituting accurate dates. Have volunteers write today's and tomorrow's weather on the chart in complete sentences. Read aloud the sentences in the Language Focus box and then together add information about yesterday's weather to the chart on the board.

Activity 6: Analyze

1. *Part a.* Together read the temperature on the thermometer on page 88. (Answer: 78 degrees Fahrenheit)

2. Write this sentence on the board: *It was _____ degrees Fahrenheit in _____ on February 23.* Then have students write sentences about the temperature in the six cities on page 89. Volunteers can read their sentences aloud for the class to compare.

(Continued on page 89.)

Language Focus

Yesterday it *was cloudy.*

   . . . *rained*
   . . . *snowed*
   . . . *was sunny*
   . . . *was windy*

5. Describe

Classwork. Tell about the weather in your area.

Yesterday	Today	Tomorrow
Date: *October 24* It rained. It was cold.	Date: *October 25* It's raining. It's cold.	Date: *October 26* It's going to rain. It's going to be cold.

6. Analyze

a. Classwork. Read the thermometers on the next page. What was the temperature in each city on February 23?

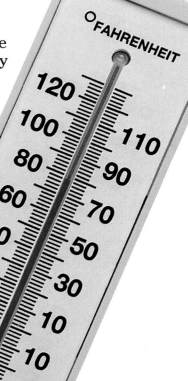

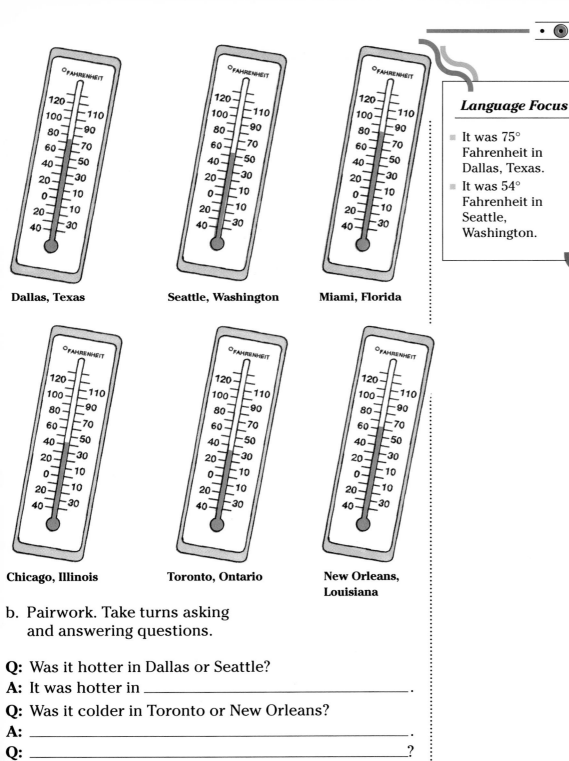

Dallas, Texas

Seattle, Washington

Miami, Florida

Chicago, Illinois

Toronto, Ontario

New Orleans, Louisiana

> ### *Language Focus*
>
> - It was 75°
>   Fahrenheit in
>   Dallas, Texas.
> - It was 54°
>   Fahrenheit in
>   Seattle,
>   Washington.

b. Pairwork. Take turns asking
   and answering questions.

Q: Was it hotter in Dallas or Seattle?

A: It was hotter in _____ .

Q: Was it colder in Toronto or New Orleans?

A: _____ .

Q: _____ ?

A: _____ .

Activity 6: Analyze *(continued)*

3. *Part b.* Model the activity by taking turns asking and answering questions with a partner. Then have pairs work together to compare temperatures in the different cities.

4. Extend the activity by having the pairs write three questions, using the model in the book. Pairs can then exchange papers and write answers. Have pairs exchange papers again and check the answers. Let pairs read their questions aloud and call on a classmate to answer.

Activity 7: Solve

1. *Part a.* Introduce the activity by asking students to compare the two thermometers on this page. Volunteers can read the temperature on each thermometer while you write their answers on the board. (Answers may vary. It was 66 degrees Fahrenheit in Los Angeles on February 23. It was 28 degrees Celsius in Rio de Janeiro.) Together read the information in the Measuring Air Temperature box.

2. Together follow the steps to convert the temperatures. You might, for example, have one student read the steps aloud while another student does the math on the board. (Answers: It was 82.4 degrees Fahrenheit in Rio de Janeiro. Thus, it was hotter in Rio de Janeiro. It was 18.8 degrees Celsius in Los Angeles.)

(Continued on page 91.)

7. **Solve**

a. Classwork. Was it hotter in Los Angeles, California, or Rio de Janeiro, Brazil? Follow these steps to find out:

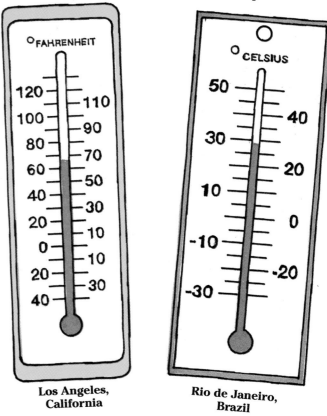

Los Angeles, California   **Rio de Janeiro, Brazil**

Temperature on February 23

Measuring Air Temperature

In most countries in the world, people use the Celsius (*Centigrade*) scale to measure air temperature.

In the United States, people use the *Fahrenheit* scale to measure air temperature.

0° Celsius = 32° Fahrenheit.

Steps:

1. Convert the temperature of Rio de Janeiro to Fahrenheit.

> *To convert Celsius to Fahrenheit*
>   a. Multiply the temperature by 9.
>   b. Divide by 5.
>   c. Add 32.

2. Compare the temperatures in Rio de Janeiro and Los Angeles.

3. Check your answer. Convert the temperature of Los Angeles to Celsius.

> **To convert Fahrenheit to Celsius**
> a. Subtract 32 from the temperature.
> b. Multiply by 5.
> c. Divide by 9.

4. Compare the temperatures in Los Angeles and Rio de Janeiro.

b. Groupwork. Put these cities in order from the hottest to the coldest.

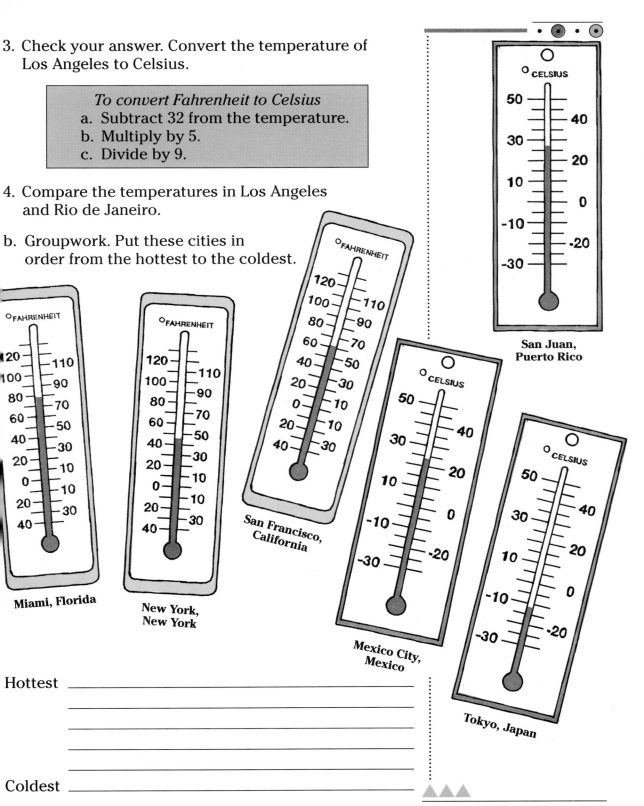

Miami, Florida

New York, New York

San Francisco, California

Mexico City, Mexico

San Juan, Puerto Rico

Tokyo, Japan

Hottest _____

_____

_____

_____

_____

Coldest _____

3. *Part b.* Together read the temperature in each city. Make sure students use the correct scale when they report the temperature. (Because the thermometers are small, the temperature readings may vary. The following readings have been used to make the conversions: Miami: 79 degrees F; New York: 45 degrees F; San Francisco: 62 degrees F; San Juan: 27 degrees C; Mexico City: 24 degrees C; Tokyo: –8 degrees C.)

4. To do this activity, students must convert all temperatures to either Fahrenheit or Celsius. Put students in groups to do the conversions. They should then put the temperatures in order from hottest to coldest. Have each group report its results. Model reading of numbers with decimals. Write, *San Juan 80.6* on the board and read aloud, *San Juan, eighty point six,* pointing to the decimal point as you say *point.* (Answers: San Juan: 80.6 F; Miami: 79 F; Mexico City: 75.2 F; San Francisco: 62 F; New York: 45 F; and Tokyo: 17.6 F. Or San Juan: 27 C; Miami: 26.1 C; Mexico City: 24 C; San Francisco: 16.6 C; New York: 7.2 C; Tokyo: –8 C.)

Activity 8: Find the Average

1. Have students locate Los Angeles and New York on a U.S. map.

2. Together read the thermometers measuring the temperatures in Los Angeles and agree on answers. (Answers may vary by a degree. 1 A.M., 39 degrees Fahrenheit; 7 A.M., 44°; 1 P.M., 67°; 7 P.M., 60°.)

3. Have students compare the temperatures at different times during the day. For example, ask: *Was it hotter in the morning or evening? When was it the hottest?*

4. Ask students to read the temperatures in New York. (Answers may vary: 1 A.M., 28 degrees Fahrenheit; 7 A.M., 32°; 1 P.M., 38°; 7 P.M., 34°.) Again ask: *Was it hotter in the morning or the evening? When was it the hottest?*

5. Have students work in small groups to follow the steps on page 93. If possible, send groups to the board to do their work. Have groups compare answers and then let one group explain how they got their answers. (Answers: Los Angeles, 52.5 degrees F; New York, 33 degrees F. Students can round off their answers.)

| 8. | **Find the Average** |

Groupwork. Follow the steps below to find the average temperature for the day.

These thermometers measured the temperatures in Los Angeles and New York at different times during one day.

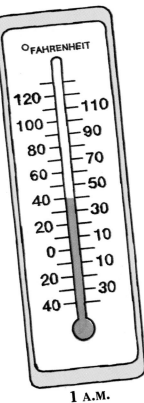

1 A.M.

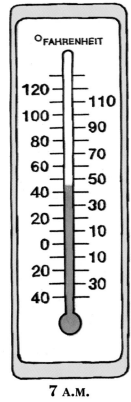

7 A.M.

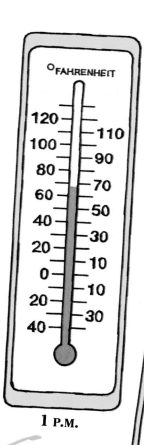

1 P.M.

7 P.M.

1 A.M.

7 A.M.

1 P.M.

7 P.M.

New York

New York

Steps:

1. Add the four temperatures in Los Angeles.
2. Divide the result by four.
3. Add the four temperatures in New York.
4. Divide the result by four.
5. Write your answers below.

    The average temperature in Los Angeles was _____.

    The average temperature in New York was _____.

Activity 9: Read a Chart

1. Before introducing this activity, review the names of the months. Encourage students to talk about the weather in your area or in their native countries at different times during the year. For example, *It's usually hot here in August.*

2. Read aloud the caption above the chart. Then have students take turns reading the temperatures in the chart. For example, *In Los Angeles, the average temperature in January was 56 degrees Fahrenheit.*

3. Draw on the board the sentence options below the chart. Together see how many sentences you can make. (Answers: In January the average monthly temperature was higher in Los Angeles. In January the average monthly temperature was lower in New York. April—higher in Los Angeles or lower in New York; July—higher in New York or lower in Los Angeles; October—higher in Los Angeles or lower in New York.) Let volunteers answer the questions at the end of the activity.

Activity 10: Read a Graph

1. Have students study the line graph on page 95 together. Ask them to read the title and find the horizontal and vertical axes. Together identify the information on each axis. (Answers: The horizontal axis shows the months. The vertical axis shows degrees in Fahrenheit.) Let volunteers tell about the temperature in New York and Los Angeles. For example, *In January the average temperature in New York was 31.8 degrees Farenheit. In January it was colder in New York.*

2. Give each student a copy of AM 5/1. Students can work on their own or with a partner to complete the line graph, using information from the chart in Activity 9.

(Continued on page 95.)

---

9. Read a Chart

Classwork. Compare the temperatures in Los Angeles and New York.

This chart shows the average monthly temperatures* in Los Angeles and New York.

City	January	April	July	October
Los Angeles	56	59.5	69	66.3
New York	31.8	51.9	76.4	57.5

*temperatures in degrees Fahrenheit

In January

In April   the average monthly temperature was higher   in Los Angeles

In July   the average monthly temperature was lower   in New York

In October

Would you rather live in Los Angeles or New York? Why?

10. Read a Graph

Classwork. Use the chart above to complete a line graph.

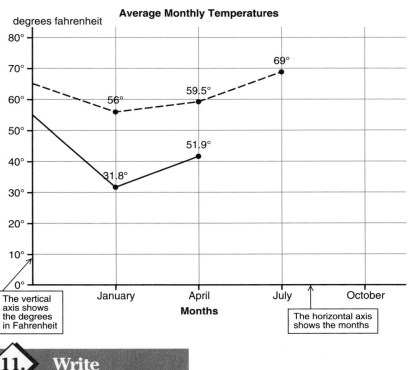

Average Monthly Temperatures

degrees fahrenheit

The vertical axis shows the degrees in Fahrenheit

The horizontal axis shows the months

Months

New York

------ Los Angeles

---

11. Write

Pairwork. Compare the average monthly temperatures in Boston, Massachusetts and Seattle, Washington. Write several sentences.

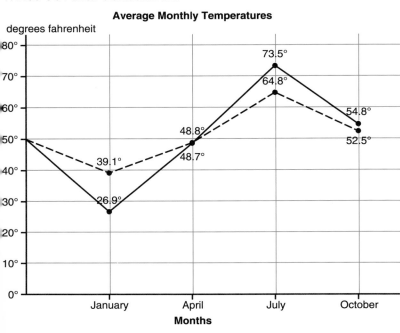

Average Monthly Temperatures

degrees fahrenheit

Months

Language Focus

- In January, it was warmer in Seattle.
- In April, it was colder in Boston.

Boston, Massachusetts

------ Seattle, Washington

---

3. Post one student's completed graph and encourage students to think about the purpose of line graphs. Ask: *Is this type of graph useful? Why? Is it easier to read than the chart? What other things could you compare on a line graph?*

4. Extend this activity by having students look in an almanac for the average monthly temperatures in U.S. cities. (Look in the index under *Temperatures*.) Have groups choose two cities and record the temperatures on a line graph.

Activity 11: Write

1. This activity requires students to read a line graph without the accompanying chart. Study the graph together focusing on the lines rather than specific temperatures. For example, ask: *In July, was it hotter in Boston or Seattle? When was it colder in Boston? In which city did the temperature change the most?*

2. Read the sentences in the Language Focus box aloud. Then have pairs work together to write several sentences, using the information in the graph.

3. Have pairs read their sentences aloud. Ask the rest of the class to raise their hands if they agree with their classmates' sentences.

4. Introduce the words *increase* and *decrease*. Show on the graph where the temperature increased and decreased. For example, *Between January and April the average temperature in Boston increased. Between July and October it decreased.*

Activity 12: Make a Line Graph

1. *Part a.* In this activity, pairs create an ideal city and choose the type of weather they would like in their city. Model the activity by telling about the type of weather you like at different times of the year. Add the temperatures in your ideal city to a chart on the board.

2. Have pairs copy the chart on page 96 and then add the temperatures in their ideal city. Encourage them to name their city.

3. *Part b.* On a large piece of paper, draw a graph similar to those in Activities 10 and 11. Each pair can then add the temperatures in their ideal city, using a different colored pencil or marker. Record the colors and the city names in a key.

4. Have groups compare temperatures in the different cities.

Activity 13: Investigate

Part a. Together describe the clothing of the two people in the picture. Introduce the terms *light-colored clothing* and *dark-colored clothing*. Read the question in the instruction line aloud. Then have pairs write their prediction on another piece of paper. Collect the predictions to use later.

(Continued on page 97.)

12. Make a Line Graph

a. Pairwork. Imagine a city. Give it a name. What do you want the weather to be like? Choose the average monthly temperatures. Write them in a chart.

This chart gives the average monthly temperatures*
in _____ .
(name of your imaginary city)

City	January	April	July	October

*temperatures in degrees Fahrenheit

b. Groupwork. Add your average monthly temperatures to a class line graph. Then compare temperatures in your ideal cities.

13. Investigate

a. Pairwork. On a hot day, do you feel cooler in dark-colored clothes or light-colored clothes? Choose a or b.

Our prediction:

a. You feel cooler in light-colored clothes.

b. You feel cooler in dark-colored clothes.

b. Classwork. Test your prediction. Try this investigation on a sunny day:

Materials: two room or outdoor thermometers, sheets of black paper and white paper of the same size and thickness

Steps:

1. Find a room with a sunny window. Measure the air temperature in the room.
2. Put the thermometers in a sunny place.
3. Cover one thermometer with white paper. Cover the other thermometer with black paper. Leave them for 30 minutes.
4. Remove the paper. Read the temperature. Record your data.

1. 2.

Color of Paper	Temperature at the beginning	Temperature after 30 minutes
Black		
White		

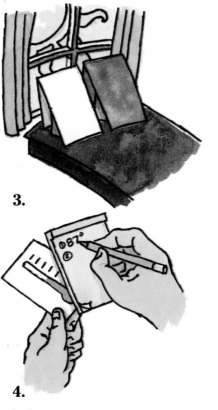

3.

4.

Part b. Borrow two thermometers from a science teacher. Read the steps and have students work together to follow the directions. Copy on the board the chart on page 97, and have students record the data on this chart.

(Continued on page 98.)

Activity 13: Investigate *(continued)*

Part c. Have volunteers put the predictions from Part a into two groups and then count the number of correct predictions. For follow up, ask students why you feel cooler in light-colored clothing. (Answer: Dark-colored clothing can soak up sunlight and turn it into heat. Light-colored clothes can reflect the heat without getting hotter.)

Activity 14: Match

Part a. Have students locate these five places, using the map on pages 104–105 or another world map.

1. *Parts b, c, and d.* Read aloud the sentences in the Language Focus box and let students add their ideas.

2. Read aloud the questions in Part b. Put students into groups to guess answers to these questions. They should record their ideas on another piece of paper.

3. Have groups compare ideas and then together check the facts on page 99.

4. Write the adjectives *hot, cold, windy, sunny, wet,* and *dry* on the board. Next to each word write the superlative form: *hottest, coldest, windiest, sunniest, wettest,* and *driest.* Give students time to study these words, and then together infer the rules for forming superlatives.

Language Focus

The hottest place on earth is _____ .
The coldest place is _____ .

---

c. Pairwork. Was your prediction correct?

14. **Match**

a. Classwork. Find these places on the map on pages 104–105.

- Antarctica
- Ethiopia, Africa
- Sahara Desert, Africa
- United States, North America
- Chile, South America

b. Groupwork. Guess the answers to these questions. Choose places from the list above.

1. Where is the hottest place on earth?
2. Where is the coldest place on earth?.
3. Where is the windiest place on earth?
4. Where is the sunniest place on earth?
5. Where is the wettest place?
6. Where is the driest place?

c. Compare answers with your classmates.

d. Check the facts on page 99.

Answers:

15. Predict

Classwork. Read this information and make a prediction.

In the story below, the wind and sun argue about something. Study the pictures and tell what you think they argue about.

Maybe they argue about ....

16. Reader's Theater

Classwork. Listen to the story.

The North Wind and the Sun

NARRATOR: One day, the north wind and the sun got into an argument.

NORTH WIND: I'm stronger than you.

Activity 15: Predict

1. Write this title on the board: *An Argument.* Under it write this dialogue: *A: That's my book. B: No, it's not. It's my book.* Read the dialogue aloud with appropriate intonation and then let two students read it aloud. Then ask the class: *What are they arguing about?* Give other examples to help students understand the meaning of the word *argue.*

2. Together read the title of the story in Activity 16 and study the pictures on pages 99—101. Have students describe what they see in each picture while you act as a consultant, helping with unfamiliar words.

3. Read the instruction line aloud and together brainstorm possible ways to complete the sentence. (They should not write in the book.)

Activity 16: Reader's Theater

1. Play the tape or read the fable aloud. Use intonation and emphasis to make the story come alive. Read the fable again, demonstrating the actions of the characters in the story.

(Continued on page 100.)

Activity 16: Reader's Theater *(continued)*

2. Let students create their own list of unfamiliar words in the story. Write this question on the board: *What does the word _____ mean?* Students can use this question as they ask about words in the story. Work together to figure out the meaning of each word, using context clues, a classmate's definition, and/or a dictionary.

SUN: Impossible! I'm much stronger than you.

NORTH WIND: Never! I am stronger.

NARRATOR: Just then, the north wind saw a traveler walking on the road below.

NORTH WIND: Let's test our strength on that traveler. I'm sure I can make her take off her coat faster than you can.

SUN: Impossible. I'm certain to win.

NARRATOR: The north wind tried first. He blew down hard on the traveler. He blew harder and harder, but the traveler held onto her coat.

SUN: Now it's my turn.

NARRATOR: At first, the sun shone gently on the traveler, who soon unbuttoned her coat. Then the sun shone in full strength. Before long, the traveler took off her coat and continued her journey without it.

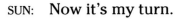

17. Share ideas

Classwork. Share ideas about the story with your classmates. Here are some questions to think about.

1. What was the argument about?
2. The wind and the sun showed their strength in different ways. How?
3. This Reader's Theater is based on a fable—a story that teaches a lesson. What lesson do you think this fable is trying to teach?

Activity 17: Share Ideas

1. Give students the opportunity to first share their ideas about the story. Encourage them to formulate their own questions and tell what they liked about the story.

2. Read the questions aloud. To give more students a chance to talk, you might want to have students discuss the questions in small groups and then report their ideas to the class. (Answers: 1. Who was stronger 2. The wind blew very hard. The sun first shone gently and later in full strength. 3. Possible answer: Gentleness works better than force.)

Activity 18: Reader's Theater

1. Show the class different kinds of maps, for example, a world map and a city map. Have them consider the purpose of maps. What do they help you to do? Write the words *story map* on the board and ask students what this type of map might help them to do.

2. Put students in groups of 3 or 4 and give each group a copy of AM 5/2. Have students look at the story map while you read the questions aloud. Then give the groups time to complete the maps. Have the groups post their maps on a classroom wall and together compare ideas. (Possible answers: What did they decide to do? They decided to test their strength on a traveler. What did the North Wind do? He blew hard on a traveler. What happened? The traveler held onto her coat. What did the Sun do? She shone gently and then in full strength. What happened? The traveler took off her coat.)

Activity 19: Roleplay

Put students in groups of three or four and let them choose roles (narrator, wind, sun, traveler). Note that the traveler does not have a speaking part so you might give this person the added responsibility of director. Give students time to practice reading the script while you circulate to model expressive reading and to support students who may have difficulty. Then have groups perform for the class.

18. Reader's Theater

Groupwork. Make a story map.

Title: The North Wind and the Sun

Problem

> **What was the problem?**
> *The wind said he was stronger.*
> *The sun said she was stronger.*

Plot (What happened?)

> **What did they decide to do?**
> *They decided to* _____
> _____

> **What did the North Wind do?**
> *He blew hard on the traveler.*

> **What did the Sun do?**
> _____
> _____

> **What happened?**
> _____
> _____

> **What happened?**
> _____
> _____

19. Roleplay

Groupwork. Get together in groups of three. Practice reading the story "The North Wind and the Sun." Then act it out for your classmates.

Activity Menu

Choose one of the following activities to do.

1. What's the weather?
Collect pictures (photographs or copies of paintings) that show different kinds of weather. Write captions for the pictures and display them.

2. Be a Weather Forecaster
Watch a TV weather forecaster. What props does the forecaster use? What information does this person give? Use what you learn to make a weather forecast to your classmates.

3. Collect Weather Songs
Think of a song about the weather. Write down the words in English or another language. Read the words to your classmates. Tell them what the song means.

4. Stay Cool
Wearing light-colored clothing can help you to stay cool. What are some other ways to stay cool in hot weather? And how can you stay warm in cold weather? Make a chart listing ways to stay cool and keep warm. Present your suggestions to the class.

5. Keep a Weather Journal
Record each day's weather in a notebook. Draw columns for the date, temperature, and weather conditions.

6. Graph the Temperature in Your Area
Look in an almanac for the average monthly temperatures of U.S. cities. (Look in the index under *Temperatures.*) Choose a city in your area and make a line graph of the temperatures. Each month, compare the actual temperature to the average temperature on your graph.

DATE	TEMP.	WEATHER CONDITIONS
May 1	45-60	Warm and sunny. No clouds. Great!

Activity Menu

Read the activities to the class and answer any questions. Then have students individually or in small groups select a project for a class or homework assignment. Projects can later be shared with the class and/or displayed in the classroom.

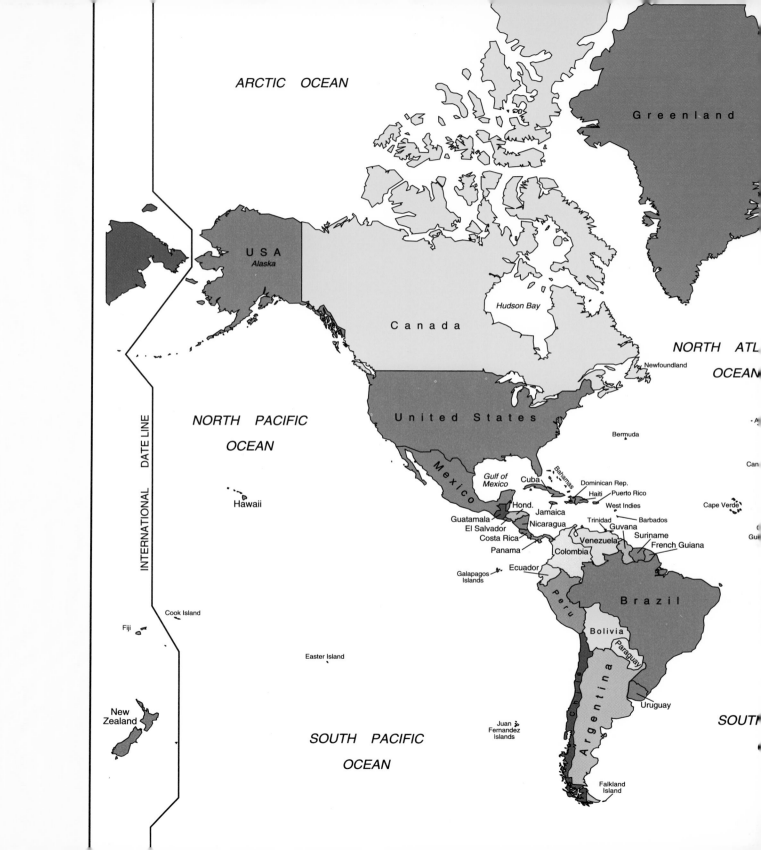

ARCTIC OCEAN

Greenland

USA
Alaska

Canada

Hudson Bay

NORTH ATL
OCEAN

Newfoundland

NORTH PACIFIC

OCEAN

INTERNATIONAL DATE LINE

Bermuda

Can

Mexico

Gulf of Mexico

Cuba

Bahamas

Dominican Rep.

Haiti   Puerto Rico

Hawaii

Hond.

West Indies

Cape Verde

Guatamala

Jamaica

Trinidad

Barbados

El Salvador

Nicaragua

Guyana

Gui

Costa Rica

Venezuela

Suriname

Panama

Colombia

French Guiana

Galapagos
Islands

Ecuador

Peru

Brazil

Cook Island

Bolivia

Fiji

Paraguay

Easter Island

Argentina

New
Zealand

Chile

Uruguay

Juan
Fernandez
Islands

SOUTH PACIFIC

OCEAN

SOUT

Falkland
Island

Making Journeys

Svalbard · Sweden · Norway · Finland · Russian Federation · Estonia · Latvia · Lithuania · Denmark · Neth. · Germany · Poland · Byelarus · Lux. · Ukraine · Moldova · Hung. · Rom. · Bul. · Black Sea · Georgia · Kazakhstan · Mongolia · N. Korea · S. Korea · Japan · Turkey · Caspian Sea · Armenia · Azerbaijan · Turkmenistan · Uzbekistan · Kyrgystan · Tajikistan · China · Greece · Cyprus · Syria · Lebanon · Israel · Iraq · Iran · Afghanistan · Pakistan · Nepal · Bhutan · Bonin Island · Ryuku Island · Mediterranean Sea · Tunisia · Libya · Egypt · Jordan · Kuwait · Bahrain · Qatar · Saudi Arabia · U.A.E. · Oman · India · Laos · Burma · Taiwan · Mariana · Niger · Chad · Sudan · Yemen · Djibouti · Bangladesh · Thai. · Vietnam · Cam. · Guam · Nigeria · Central African Republic · Ethiopia · Somalia · Philippines · Benin · Uganda · Sri Lanka · Brunei · Caroline Islands · Cameroon · Rwanda · Kenya · Malasia · Papua New Guinea · Gabon · Congo Rep. · Zaire · Burundi · Tanzania · Singapore · Indonesia · New Guinea · Malawi · Angola · Zambia · Comoros · Madagascar · Mozambique · Solomon Islands · Namibia · Zimb. · Mauritius · Réunion · Bots. · Swaziland · Australia · Lord Howe · South Africa · Lesotho · INDIAN OCEAN · Tasmania

1. List

a. Classwork. What countries have you lived in or visited? List them on the board.

Student text pages 104–105 and 106

Activity 1: List

1. *Part a.* Model this activity by naming the countries you have lived in or visited. Point to these countries on a map and then list them on the board. Let a volunteer follow your example, identifying the countries she or he has lived in or visited.

2. Give students time to find the countries they have lived in or visited, using the map in the book. Then have them take turns naming the countries while a volunteer lists them on the board. Save this list to use later.

3. *Part b.* Together study the chart on page 106. Ask students to find Zaire, Laos, and Canada on the map on pages 104–105. Then read the sentences in the Language Focus box on page 106 aloud and let volunteers point to these three continents on the map. Have students name other countries in each of these continents.

4. Have students locate the remaining four continents, using a wall map or a globe. (Note that Antarctica is not on the map on pages 104–105.) Write these sentences on the board: _____ is in Europe. _____ is in South America. Let volunteers complete the sentences. Once students have identified each continent, ask them to define the word *continent* (a large mass of land).

5. Copy on the board the chart on page 106. Tell students that they are going to classify or group the countries in their list from Part a. Then have students take turns reporting information. For example, *Venezuela is in South America.* Let another student record this information in the appropriate column in the chart.

(Continued on page 106.)

Activity 1: List (continued)

6. Go over the information in the chart with the class. *Where is Canada? Where is Laos?* Point out that in their answers they can substitute the pronoun *it* for the name of a country. For example, *It's in South America.* Then have them identify the continents that no one in the class has visited.

7. Review comparatives by asking questions about the continents. For example, *Which continent is larger, Africa or Asia? Is Europe smaller than North America?* Together put the continents in order from largest to smallest. (Answer: Asia, Africa, North America, South America, Antarctica, Europe, and Australia.) (Because of the projection used, the map on pages 104–105 does not accurately reflect the relative sizes of continents and countries. Use of a globe is recommended if possible.)

Activity 2: Identify

1. *Part a.* Read the captions aloud while students look at the pictures. Tell students how you usually come to school. For example, *I usually come to school by car.* Then let volunteers tell how they come to school.

2. Together study the chart on page 107. Read the first question aloud: *How can you get from Italy to Brazil?* Read the answers aloud, using the model in the upper Language Focus box on page 107. Then have students find these two countries on a map and check the answers. Read the second question aloud: *How can you get from Canada to Mexico?* Let volunteers answer and trace the route on a map.

3. Give each student a copy of AM 6/1 or have them copy the chart on page 107. Working as a class or in pairs, students can add their answers to the chart. Encourage them to refer to the map on pages 104–105 as they complete the chart.

(Continued on page 107.)

---

b. Classwork. Group the countries on your list.

Continents of the World

Africa	Antarctica	Asia	Australia	Europe	North America	South America
Zaire		Laos			Canada	

Which continents has no one in the class visited?

> **Language Focus**
>
> - Canada is in North America.
> - Laos is in Asia.
> - Zaire is in Africa.

2. **Identify**

a. Classwork. Answer the questions on page 107.

▼**By boat**   **By plane** ▶

▲ **On foot**

How can you get from . . . ?	by car	by boat	by plane	on foot
Italy to Brazil		✓	✓	
Canada to Mexico				
People's Republic of China to Turkey				
Saudi Arabia to Afghanistan				
Puerto Rico to Bolivia				
_____ to _____				

Language Focus

- You can get from Italy to Brazil by boat.
- You can't get from Italy to Brazil by car.

By bus▶

▼By car

▲ By train

b. Groupwork. Write three questions. Then read your questions to another group.

Can you get from _____ *to* _____ *by* _____ ?

c. Groupwork. Add the names of countries to this chant. Then read your chant to the class.

Getting There

You can get from _____ to _____ by boat,

but you can't get there by _____ .

You can get from _____ to _____ by car,

but you can't get there by _____ .

You can get from _____ to _____ by plane,

but you can't get there by boat.

Language Focus

Q: Can you get from India to Korea by boat?
A: Yes, you can.
Q: Can you get from Australia to Mexico by car?
A: No, you can't.

▲▲▲

Activity 2: Identify *(continued)*

4. Students can take turns reporting their answers, using *can* and *can't*. For example, *You can get from Puerto Rico to Bolivia by plane. You can't get from Puerto Rico to Bolivia by car.*

5. Have students work in pairs or small groups to add their own questions to the chart. For example, *How can you get from Korea to France?* Have them read their questions aloud for the rest of the class to answer.

6. *Part b.* Read the questions in the lower Language Focus box on page 107 aloud, and let a volunteer read the answers. Write this question on the board: *Can you get from* _____ *to* _____ *by* _____ ? Add the names of two countries to the question and let students answer.

7. Put students in small groups to write their own questions on another piece of paper, using the questions in the Language Focus box as models.

8. Have the groups exchange papers and answer the questions. Encourage them to refer to a map for information. Groups can then read the questions and their answers aloud for the class to check.

9. Read the chant "Getting There" aloud, substituting the sound *hmmm* for the blank lines. For example, *You can get from hmmm to hmmm by hmmm.* Then have students work in groups to write a completed chant on another piece of paper. As with other chants, keep a steady beat, alternating 4 and 3 beats per line. Because some country names have many syllables (e.g., The United States) the beats should be a little slower than in the earlier chants.

10. Have groups exchange chants and check for accuracy. Give them time to practice reading the chants in their groups and then have them read to the class. As groups read their chants, volunteers can point to the places on a wall map.

Activity 3: Evaluate

1. *Parts a and b.* Review the adjectives on page 108 by together completing a chart like this on the board:

traveling by car

Advantages	Disadvantages
+	−

Help students to come up with some of the advantages or good things about traveling by car. For example, *It's cheap, fast, and comfortable*. Then have them think of the disadvantages. For example, *It's dangerous*. Add their ideas to the chart on the board. Repeat with the other forms of transportation.

2. Write *by car* and *by plane* on the board and ask: *Which is faster, traveling by car or by plane? Which is cheaper? Which is more comfortable?* Then add the words *by boat* to the list on the board. Point to the three forms of transportation and ask: *Which is the cheapest way to travel? Which is the most comfortable way to travel?*

3. Put students in groups and give each group a copy of AM 6/2 or have them copy the chart on page 108. Then give them time to answer the questions in the chart.

4. Read the example aloud. Then have groups take turns reporting their answers, using the example as a model. For example, *The slowest way to travel is on foot*. If the groups came up with different answers, encourage them to give reasons to support their answers.

(Continued on page 109.)

---

3. ▸ Evaluate

Language Focus

Q: What is *the fastest* way to travel?
A: By plane.

the fastest
the slowest
the safest
the most expensive
the most comfortable
the most dangerous
the least expensive
the least comfortable

a. Groupwork. Answer these questions. Tell what you think.

What is . . . ?	
the fastest way to travel	*by plane*
the slowest way to travel	
the most expensive way to travel	
the least expensive way to travel	
the safest way to travel	
the most dangerous way to travel	
the most comfortable way to travel	
the least comfortable way to travel	

b. Report your group's answers to the class.

Example:
The fastest way to travel is __by plane__ .

c. Pairwork. Think about a trip you took. Then take turns asking and answering the questions below.

Example: Q: When did you take this trip?
A: __*Last year*__ .
Q: Where did you go?
A: __*To New York*__ .
Q: How did you get there?
A: __*By bus*__ .

d. Write a sentence about your partner's trip. Then read the sentence to the class.

Example:
Last year, my partner went to New York by bus.

4. ▸ Preview

Classwork. Study the pictures on pages 110-112. How can you travel across the continent of Antarctica? Share ideas with your classmates.

You can travel	You can't travel
on foot	*by car*

5. ▸ Describe

a. Classwork. Look again at the pictures on pages 110-112. Then choose the words below that describe Antarctica.

cold

hot

crowded   empty

Language Focus

- You can travel on foot.
- You can't travel by car.

mountainous

flat

forested

treeless

Unit Six Making Journeys **109**

---

5. *Parts c and d.* Copy on the board the three questions in the example. Tell students that you are thinking about a trip you took and get them to ask the three questions. Have a volunteer write your answers on the board. Ask a volunteer to think about a trip and then answer the three questions. Record this student's answers on the board. Write a sentence about this student's trip, using the model in Part d. For example, *Last year, Sami went to San Diego by car.* Have the class look back at your answers and write a sentence about your trip.

6. Have students get together in pairs to interview each other. Then have them write a sentence about their partner's trip. Students can read their sentences aloud while the rest of the class finds the places on a map.

Activity 4: Preview

1. Have students find Antarctica on a world map. Encourage volunteers to share what they already know about this continent.

2. Give students time to study the pictures of Antarctica on pages 110–112 while you draw on the board the chart in Activity 4. Read the sentences in the Language Focus box on page 109 aloud and then have students add other examples to the chart.

Activity 5: Describe

1. *Part a.* Together study the pictures on this page and read the one-word descriptions. Then have students look again at the pictures of Antarctica on pages 110–112. Write this sentence starter on the board: *Antarctica is _____.* Students can complete the sentence using words from page 109. Make sure that students understand that Antarctica is flat in some places and mountainous in other places. (Answers: cold, empty, mountainous (in places), treeless, and flat (in places).

(Continued on page 110.)

▲▲▲   **109**

Activity 5: Describe *(continued)*

2. *Part b.* Draw the diagram on the board. Have volunteers come to the board to add the words from Part a and any other ideas from the pictures or from their background knowledge.

Activity 6: Shared Reading

1. Use the pictures on pages 110–112 to help prepare students for the reading. Together look over each picture carefully and let students describe what they see. Help them with unfamiliar words and write them on the board. Encourage students to ask questions about the pictures and have a volunteer write them on the board. For example, *Who are the people with the peace sign?* They can look for answers to these questions as they read the article.

2. Have students look at the map of Antarctica on page 111. Explain that a group of six people traveled across Antarctica in 1989. The red line shows their route across the continent. Have them locate the flat areas and the mountainous areas on their route. Using the mileage marker in the key, students can estimate the distance that they traveled. Ask more proficient students to predict the difficulties these travelers had on their trip. List their ideas on the board.

3. Read the first paragraph of the article aloud. Then ask students to read it again, looking for information to add to the diagram in Activity 5. (icy, windy) Have students use context clues to guess the meaning of the word *recorded*. Read aloud this sentence from the first paragraph: *Ice more than a mile thick covers 98 percent of the land.* Then ask students to measure the thickness of their textbook. Explain that there are 12 inches in a foot and 5,280 feet in a mile.

(Continued on page 111.)

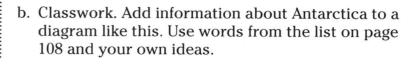

b. Classwork. Add information about Antarctica to a diagram like this. Use words from the list on page 108 and your own ideas.

What's the weather like?

What's the landscape like?

Antarctica

What lives in Antarctica?

6. **Shared Reading**

Read about Antarctica and add more ideas to your diagram.

Crossing Antarctica

Antarctica, the land of the South Pole, is the world's coldest, iciest, and windiest continent. Scientists have recorded a temperature of minus 128.6°F (−89.2°C) in Antarctica! Ice more than a mile thick covers 98 percent of the land. Along the coast, scientists have recorded winds of up to 200 miles (322 kilometers) an hour.

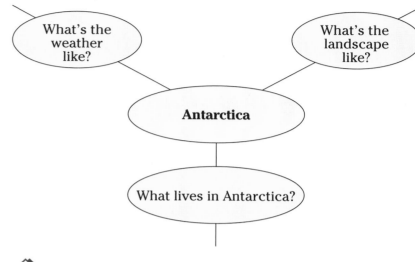

Almost no life can exist in the interior of Antarctica. Along its shores and in the surrounding waters, however, a variety of wildlife lives. Penguins, seals, whales, and many kinds of fish swim in the ocean surrounding Antarctica.

In 1989, a six-person team spent 221 days traveling across the continent of Antarctica. The team included scientists and explorers from the former Soviet Union, China, Japan, France, Britain, and the United States. They traveled across the continent on cross-country skis while 36 dogs pulled their equipment.

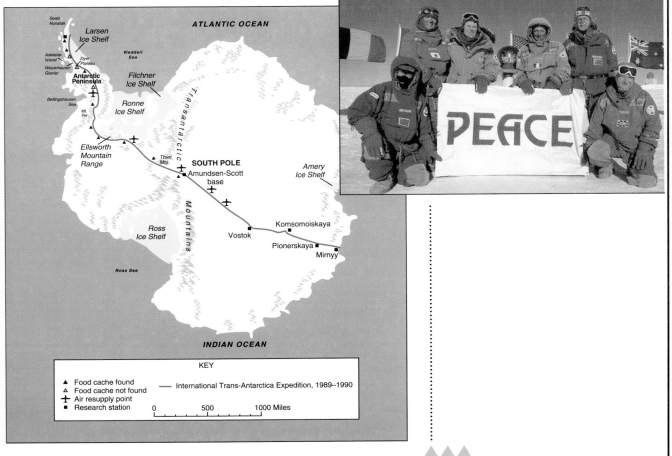

KEY

▲ Food cache found
△ Food cache not found
╋ Air resupply point
■ Research station

—— International Trans-Antarctica Expedition, 1989–1990

0   500   1000 Miles

Activity 6: Shared Reading (continued)

4. There are a number of ways you can handle the remainder of the reading, on pages 111 and 112, depending on the abilities of your class. With more proficient students, you might choose to play the tape recorded version of the story or let students read on their own. Encourage them to look for answers to their questions on the board as they read. With less proficient students, you might want to read a paragraph aloud and then stop and together share what you learned.

5. Together add ideas from the reading to the diagram in Activity 5. Students can then use the diagram to report what they learned about Antarctica.

6. Instead of asking a list of prefabricated questions, encourage students to talk about what they learned and what interested them. You can get the discussion started by telling about something that interested you.

Activity 7: Analyze

1. *Part a.* Have students number a piece of paper from 1 to 6. Write the words *Agree* and *Disagree* on the board. Read the first statement aloud and ask students if they agree or disagree. Have them write their answer next to number 1. Students can work on their own to analyze the remaining sentences.

2. *Part b.* Have students get together in groups to compare answers. Then let the groups take turns reporting answers. (Answers: 1. Disagree; 2. Agree; 3. Disagree; 4. Agree; 5. Disagree; 6. Agree.) Ask students to make the false statements true.

3. Follow up by having students write their own true/false statements based on the article, and share them with the class.

The team traveled an average of 17 miles a day. Sometimes, the traveling was difficult and dangerous. Strong winds and snow made it difficult to see and the explorers worried about getting lost. They also had to cross an area with crevasses in the ice. Many times, the dogs fell into these deep holes and the explorers had to pull them out.

"It's really like another planet," said one team member. "The weather is always trying to kill you. It's typically 30 degrees below zero with winds of 30 miles per hour. That's a common day."

7. Analyze

a. On your own. Tell if you agree or disagree with the statements below.

1. It's colder in North America than in Antarctica.
2. Ice covers much of Antarctica.
3. There aren't any animals in Antarctica.
4. Traveling across Antarctica is dangerous.
5. You can travel across Antarctica by car.
6. A crevasse is a deep hole.

b. Compare ideas with your classmates.

8. Evaluate

a. Groupwork. The explorers took the items below on their trip across Antarctica. Put these items into two groups.

Necessities (things you need to stay alive in Antarctica)	Luxuries (things you don't need to stay alive)
food	camera

Cooking stove ▼

Parka ▶

◀ **Bandages**

◀ **Matches**

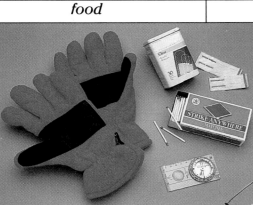

Gloves ▲   **Compass ▲**

▲
Sleeping bag

▲ Tent

▼ Food

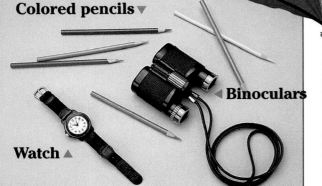

Colored pencils ▼

◀ **Binoculars**

Watch ▲

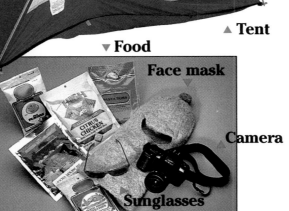

Face mask

Camera

Sunglasses

Activity 8: Evaluate

1. *Parts a and b.* Before students look at the pictures, write this question on the board: *What did the explorers take on their trip across Antarctica?* Encourage students to get ideas from the reading and the photographs on pages 110–112. List their ideas on the board.

2. Together study the pictures on page 113. Tell them that these are some other things the explorers took on their trip. Have students read the labels and tell what you can use each item for.

3. Draw on the board the chart on page 113 and give examples to illustrate the difference between necessities and luxuries.

4. Put students in groups to classify the pictured items. Then have the groups copy their charts on the board. Together look for similarities and differences in the charts and let the groups explain their choices.

(Continued on page 114.)

Activity 8: Evaluate *(continued)*

5. *Part c.* Copy on the board the chart on page 114. Then model the activity with a partner. Read aloud the first question in the chart or Language Focus box, and let your partner read the answer. Get your partner to ask the second question, and then give your answer.

6. Pair students and ask them to copy the chart on page 114. Instruct them to add several more items to the chart, choosing from the pictures on page 113. Then give them time to add their answers to the chart.

7. Have pairs take turns asking a question from the chart. Other pairs can report their answer.

Activity 9: Compute

Part a. Read the two questions aloud and then ask students to look back at the reading to find the answers. Have them compare answers and show where in the article they found the information. (Answers: 1. 221 days; 2. 17 miles.)

Part b. Read the question aloud and then write the formula *d* = *rt* on the board. Read the formula aloud (distance equals rate multiplied by the time) and ask what information they already know (the rate and the time). Have students substitute these numbers in the formula. (*d*=17 x 221) and calculate the answer. (Answer: 3,757 miles) Compare this answer to their predictions, using the mileage marker in the map key.

b. Share ideas with your classmates.

c. Pairwork. Why did the explorers take these items on their trip? Write your ideas in a chart. Then compare ideas with your classmates.

Language Focus

Q: Why did they take tents?
A: To stay warm at night.

Why did they take . . . ?	
tents	*To stay warm at night*
binoculars	
sleeping bags	
colored pencils	

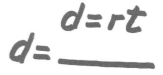

9. Compute

a. On your own. Look back at the reading to find answers to these questions:

1. How many days did it take to cross Antarctica?

2. How many miles did the explorers travel each day?

b. How many miles did the explorers travel in all? Use the formula below to find the answer.

Formula: Distance equals rate (number of miles per day) multiplied by the time.

$$d = rt$$
$$d = \underline{\qquad}$$

10. Plan

a. Groupwork. Traveling across Antarctica on skis is challenging, or difficult to do. Follow the instructions below to plan another challenging trip.

1. Choose a place for your trip. Draw your route on a map.
2. Describe this area in a chart like this:

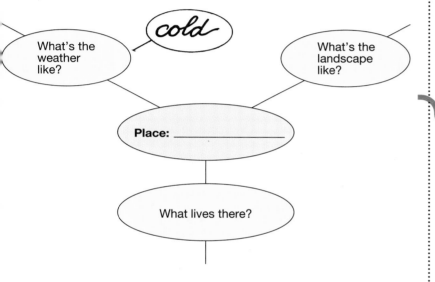

What's the weather like?

cold

What's the landscape like?

Place: _____

What lives there?

Language Focus

- We will travel by boat.
- We will take a tent.

3. Answer the questions in a chart like this.

How will you travel?	
What will you take with you?	
What will be challenging about your trip?	

b. Share your plan with the class. Each person in your group can tell something about your plan.

Activity 10: Plan

1. *Part a.* Ask students to explain why the Antarctica trip was challenging or difficult. List their ideas on the board.

2. Tell students that they are going to plan another challenging trip. Together brainstorm some examples of challenging trips (traveling down the Nile River in a kayak, crossing Canada on foot, crossing the Atlantic Ocean in a sailboat) and then choose one example to use as a model.

3. Copy on the board the diagram on page 115 and write your example in the center circle. Then have students add information to the diagram.

4. Copy on the board the chart on page 115 and have the class work together to add answers.

5. Put students in groups to plan their own challenging trip. Give each group a copy of AM 6/3 and have them record their ideas on the diagram and chart.

6. *Part b.* Have each group present its trip to the class. Give them time in advance to prepare their presentation. Each person in a group should contribute, but they can decide how to divide up the work. At the end of the presentations, let the class choose the most challenging trip. Review superlatives by also choosing the <u>most dangerous</u> trip, the <u>safest</u> trip, the <u>longest</u> trip, etc.

Activity 11: List

1. *Part a.* Model the activity by listing on the board the states that you have lived in or visited. Give students time to make their own lists. (If your students have not traveled in the United States, you can instead ask students to list the states that begin with the letter *m*.) They can then take turns reading their lists while another student adds the places to the list on the board. Together locate each state on a U.S. map. Keep this list on the board to use later.

2. Have students find Alaska and Hawaii on a wall map or globe and explain that these two states are part of the United States. Ask how you can get to these two states from your town or city.

3. Review superlatives by asking students to find the largest and smallest states. (Answer: Largest—Alaska, Second largest—Texas, Smallest—Rhode Island)

(Continued on page 118.)

11. List

a. **Classwork.** Which states in the United States have you lived in or visited? List them on the board.

Canada

Superior

Michigan

Huron

Michigan

Erie

Ontario

Toronto

Detroit

Cleveland

Chicago

Indiana

Ohio

Indianapolis

Ohio River

West Virginia

Kentucky

Tennessee

Mississippi

Alabama

Georgia

Atlanta

South Carolina

North Carolina

Virginia

Pennsylvania

Pittsburgh

Philadelphia

New York

Ottawa

Montréal

Québec

St. Lawrence River

Connecticut River

Maine

New Hampshire

Vermont

Massachusetts

Boston

Rhode Island

Connecticut

New York

New Jersey

Delaware

Maryland

Washington, D.C.

Florida

Miami

New Orleans

United States

Activity 11: List *(continued)*

4. *Part b.* Write these terms on the board: *northern part, southern part, eastern part, western part,* and *central part.* Together find these parts of the United States, using the map on pages 116 and 117.

5. Have students find California on the map on page 116. While they are looking at the map, read the sentences about California in the Language Focus box on page 118. Write this sentence on the board: _____ *is in the western part of the United States.* Let students complete the sentence, using information from the map.

6. Ask students to tell about the states in the chart on this page. For example, *Oregon is in the northern part of the United States.* Then have them find each of these states on the U.S. map. Help students to understand that states may be in two parts of the country. For example, California is in both the western part and the southern part of the United States. Oregon is in both the western part and the northern part

7. Draw the chart on the board. Then have students group the states in their list from Part a. To do this, students can take turns reporting information while a volunteer adds the information to the chart. Together study the completed chart and answer this question: *Which part of the United States does your class know best?*

8. Extend this activity by having students add other states to each category in the chart.

9. *Parts c and d.* Have students study the map of Canada on page 119. Together list on the board the provinces that you and your students have lived in or visited.

10. Draw on the board the chart on page 118 and let the class group the provinces in their list. Together study the chart and answer this question: *Which part of Canada does your class know best?*

(Continued on page 119.)

---

b. Classwork. Group the states on your list. Most states will fit into more than one group. Then answer the question below.

The United States

North (northern part)	South (southern part)	East (eastern part)	West (western part)	Center (central part)
Oregon	*Alabama*	*New York*	*California*	*Missouri*
New York	*California*		*Oregon*	

Language Focus

- California is in the western part of the United States.
- California is in the southern part of the United States.
- California is in the southwestern part of the United States.

Which part of the United States does your class know best?

c. Classwork. Study the map on page 119. Which provinces in Canada have you lived in or visited? List them on the board.

d. Classwork. Group the provinces in Canada on your list. Then answer the question below.

Canada

North (northern part)	South (southern part)	East (eastern part)	West (western part)	Center (central part)
	Manitoba	*Quebec*		*Manitoba*

Which part of Canada does your class know best?

11. Extend this activity by asking about the cities on the map of Canada. For example, *Where is Vancouver? It's in the southwestern part of Canada.*

ELLESMERE ISLAND

QUEEN ELIZABETH ISLANDS

BANKS ISLAND

SKA (SA)

VICTORIA ISLAND

BAFFIN ISLAND

YUKON

NORTHWEST TERRITORIES

HUDSON BAY

LABRADOR

NEWFOUNDLAND

St. John's

BRITISH COLUMBIA

ALBERTA

Edmonton

SASKAT-CHEWAN

MANITOBA

QUÉBEC

Vancouver

Calgary

Saskatoon

Regina

Winnipeg

ONTARIO

Québec

NOVA SCOTIA

Halifax

Montréal

Ottawa

NEW BRUNSWICK

Toronto

United States

Activity 12: Locate

1. *Part a.* Read the instruction line aloud. Then have students find Montreal and San Diego on the map on pages 116 and 117. Ask the questions in the upper Language Focus box and let a student read the answers.

2. Let students take turns asking about the cities listed on page 120. For example, *Where's Chicago, Illinois?* Have students refer to the U.S. map on pages 116–117 to answer. For example, *It's in the central part of the United States.*

3. *Part b.* Put students in groups and give each group a copy of AM 6/4. Tell them to draw their route from Montreal to San Diego on this map. Remind them to visit the cities listed in their book and any other cities as well.

4. Have the groups answer the questions in the book and then write their answers on the board. Together compare the responses. (Students will compare their routes in the next part of the activity.)

5. *Part c.* Ask questions to find out about one group's route, using the model in the lower Language Focus box. For example, *Where will you go from Montreal?* As they answer your questions, draw their route on a copy of AM 6/4. The class can then compare the two maps to see if the routes are the same.

6. Give each group a colored pencil. Pair up the groups and tell them to add the other group's route to their map on AM 6/4. They can ask questions to get information but they cannot look at the other group's map.

7. Have the groups display their maps and tell if they took the same route from Montreal to San Diego.

Activity 13: Jigsaw

1. *Part a.* Have students look at the photograph on page 120. Together come up with questions about these two people. For example, *Where are they? Why are they carrying umbrellas? Why are they traveling on foot?*

(Continued on page 121.)

Language Focus

Q: Where's Montreal?
A: It's in the eastern part of Canada.
Q: Where's San Diego?
A: It's in the western part of the United States.

Language Focus

Q: Where will you go from Montreal?
A: From Montreal, we'll go to Ottawa, Ontario.

12. Locate

a. **Classwork.** Take a trip by car from Montreal, Quebec, to San Diego, California. Visit the cities below on your trip. Locate them on the map on pages 116-117.

- Chicago, Illinois
- Kansas City, Missouri
- Montreal, Quebec
- Ottawa, Ontario
- Phoenix, Arizona
- San Diego, California
- Santa Fe, New Mexico
- St. Paul, Minnesota

b. **Groupwork.** What route will you take from Montreal to San Diego? Draw it on a map. Then answer the questions below.

1. How many provinces in Canada will you travel through?
2. How many states in the United States will you travel through?
3. What large rivers will you cross?

c. **Compare** routes with another group.

13. Jigsaw

a. **Classwork.** In 1976, Barbara and Peter Jenkins walked from New Orleans, Louisiana, to Florence, Oregon. Find these places on the map on page 116.

b. **Pairwork.** Student A looks at page 121 only. Student B looks at page 122 only. Ask your partner for information.

Student A: Ask your partner questions to complete the
Jenkins' route from New Orleans to Florence.

Example:

You: Where did they go from ___New Orleans___ ?

Your partner: From New Orleans, they went to Westlake.

You: Where's ___Westlake___ ?

Your partner: It's in the western part of Louisiana.

2. Read the instruction line aloud and together find New Orleans and Florence on the map on pages 116–117. Have students predict the number of states that the Jenkins traveled through on their trip from New Orleans to Florence.

3. *Part b.* Put students in pairs. Designate a Student A and a Student B in each pair. Give the Student As a copy of AM 6/5. Give Student Bs a copy of AM 6/6. Explain that their map shows part of the Jenkins' route across the United States. Have them study their map and find the missing parts. Tell students that they are going to get information from a partner to complete the Jenkins route.

4. Model the activity by working with a Student B. Read the questions in the example on page 121 and let your partner answer. Add your partner's answer to the map on AM 6/5. Then ask: *Where did they go from Westlake?* Let your partner look at the map and answer. (Answer: *From Westlake they went to Dallas.*) Then let your partner ask about the route from Dallas and add your answer to his or her map.

5. If possible, have the students in each pair sit across from each other to discourage them from looking at each other's map. Circulate to make sure they understand the activity and to answer any questions.

(Continued on page 123.)

Student B: Ask your partner questions to complete the Jenkins' route from New Orleans to Florence.

Example:

You: Where did they go from _Dallas_ ?

Your partner: From Dallas they went to Olney.

You: Where's _Olney_ ?

Your partner: It's in northern Texas.

Barbara & Peter Jenkin's
Route Across The United States

Continental Divide

0 100 200 300 Kilometers
0 100 200 300 Miles

c. Compare maps with your partner. Then answer these questions:

1. How many states did they travel through?
2. Which rivers did they cross?
3. Which mountains did they cross?
4. Find the Continental Divide on the map on page 122. (It's a dotted line.)

Where did Barbara and Peter Jenkins cross the Continental Divide?

 14. Describe

a. Groupwork. Choose one picture. Find the place on the map on page 122.

These pictures show places that Barbara and Peter Jenkins visited on their trip across the United States.

The Cascade Range in Oregon between Salem and Prineville.

The Continental Divide

The Continental Divide is an imaginary line that runs along the Rocky Mountains. Most streams on the western side of this line eventually drain into the Pacific Ocean. Most streams on the eastern side drain into the Atlantic Ocean.

Activity 13: Jigsaw *(continued)*

6. *Part c.* When they have completed the route, partners can compare maps and write answers to the questions on page 123. Note that to answer question #3, students must look at a physical map of the United States. Then have pairs exchange papers and compare answers. (Answers: 1. seven states 2. Red River, Rio Grande, Colorado, Green, and Snake 3. Rocky Mountains and Cascade Range 4. They crossed the Continental Divide in Colorado.)

Activity 14: Describe

1. *Part a.* Have students look at the photographs on pages 123 and 124. Explain that these are places that Barbara and Peter Jenkins passed through on their trip across the United States.

2. Put student in groups and assign or have them choose one of the photographs. Have them find this place or area on the map on page 122.

(Continued on page 124.)

Activity 14: Describe (continued)

3. *Parts b and c.* Give each group a copy of AM 6/7 or have them copy the chart on this page. They should work together to answer the questions in the chart and take notes. If possible, have them look for more information, using library reference materials.

4. Have each group make a short presentation telling about the place in their photograph.

5. Bring to class the book *The Walk West* by Barbara and Peter Jenkins, William Morrow and Company, New York, 1981. Let students study the pictures in the book to find out more about their trip.

6. Students might want to write to Peter and Barbara Jenkins c/o the William Morrow and Company to ask questions about their trip.

7. Have students choose another place on the Jenkins' route and look for pictures of this area in library books.

The Book Cliffs in eastern Utah

Oil fields in western Texas

b. Groupwork. Write about the place in your picture.

Example:

Place: _____

Where is it?	
What's the weather like?	
What's the landscape like?	

c. Show the class where this place is on the map. Tell them about it.

Activity Menu

Choose one of the following activities to do.

1. What's it like there?

Write about a country you have lived in. Here are some questions you might answer in your writing:

- Where is this country?
- What's the weather like?
- What's the landscape like?

Share your writing with your classmates.

2. Plan a trip

Plan a trip from North America to another country far away. Tell how you can get there. Draw the route on a map. Show your route to your classmates.

3. Describe a trip

Tell your classmates about a trip you took. Show your route on a map. Tell about any problems you had. Answer any questions your classmates have.

4. Read a magazine article

In a library, find a copy of the November 1990 issue of *National Geographic* magazine. Turn to page 67 and study the pictures of the International Expedition to Antarctica. Look for information about the trip across the continent. Share what you learned with your classmates.

5. Collect information

Choose one of the states in the United States or provinces in Canada. Collect information about this state or province to share with your classmates. Study a map in an atlas. Look up information in an encyclopedia.

Activity Menu

Read the activities to the class and answer any questions. Then have students individually or in small groups select a project for a class or home-work assignment. Projects can later be shared with the class and/or displayed in the classroom.

Language Focus

- Raul couldn't understand his teachers.
- Hanh couldn't eat the _____

Solving Problems

1. Listen

a. **Classwork.** Listen and complete the sentences.

These students moved to North America last year. What problems did they have when they arrived here?

1. Raul: I couldn't understand my _____.
2. Alicia: I didn't know anyone at _____.
3. Ahmed: People couldn't say my _____.
4. Hanh: I couldn't eat the _____.
            It was very different from the _____ in my country.
5. Boris: I didn't speak _____ very well.
6. Rosalva: Sometimes I got _____.

b. Report what you learned.

Activity 1: Listen

1. *Part a.* Introduce this activity by together listing some of the problems people have when they move to a new country. For example, *Maybe they can't speak the language. Maybe they can't find a place to live.* Write the ideas on the board.

2. Read aloud the instruction line and the information about the students pictured on these pages. Together think of possible ways to complete the sentences on page 127.

3. Give each student a copy of AM 7/1 or have them copy the sentences in the book. Tell them to listen and complete each sentence. Then play the tape or read the script twice.

4. *Part b.* Read the sentences in the Language Focus box. Then let students tell about the students on this page.

Activity 2: Think–Pair–Share

1. *Part a.* Let volunteers identify some of the problems they had during their first days in this country. You can help with unfamiliar words and write their ideas on the board.

2. Have students work on their own to list some of the problems they had during their first days in this country. Circulate to answer questions.

3. *Part b.* Put students in pairs to share their stories. Tell them to listen carefully to their partner's story. Later they will tell their partner's story to other classmates.

4. *Part c.* Pair up the pairs and let students take turns telling their partner's story.

Activity 3: Predict

Read the instruction line aloud. Write the bold-faced question on the board and then list the ideas in the second Language Focus box. Let students suggest other possibilities and add them to the list.

Activity 4: Shared Reading

1. Tell students to listen for the problems Elena had on her first day at school. Then play the tape or read the story aloud. Play the tape again and let students read along.

(Continued on page 129.)

Language Focus

- I couldn't _____ .
- I didn't _____ .

Language Focus

- Maybe she got lost.
- Maybe she didn't know anyone.

2. Think-Pair-Share

a. On your own. Think about your first days in this country. What problems did you have?

b. Pairwork. Tell your partner about your first days in this country. Listen carefully to your partner's story.

c. Get together with another pair. Tell about your partner's first days in this country.

3. Predict

Classwork. The story below tells about one student's first day at a new school. What problems do you think she had? List your ideas.

What problems did she have on her first day at school?

_____

_____

_____

4. Shared Reading

My First Day at School

My first day at this school was January 15, 1992. When I got to school, I went to the office. The counselor in the office gave me a class schedule. I couldn't find my homeroom so she took me there. I was really happy in this class because all of the students spoke Spanish. When homeroom finished, my new friends helped me to find my next class. When I got to this class, there were only two students, and they didn't speak Spanish. I was really nervous because I didn't speak English very well. I tried to relax and do my best, but it wasn't easy.

At noon, I had to go to the cafeteria, but I didn't know where it was. I didn't see any Spanish-speaking students in the hallway, so I asked a teacher. He told me that the cafeteria was on the first floor. After lunch, I had three more classes. Many students spoke Russian, and I couldn't understand them. I tried to speak English with them, and they seemed friendly. After school, I went home. This was my first day in school.

—Elena

5. List

a. On your own. Where did Elena go on her first day at school? List ideas from the reading.

First, she ___*went to the office*___ .

Then, she went _____ .

Next, _____ .

After that, _____ .

After lunch, _____ .

After school, _____ .

b. Pairwork. Compare lists with your partner.

Language Focus

- First, she went to the office.
- Then, she went _____ .

6. Answer Questions

a. Pairwork. Answer the questions in a chart like this.

What problems did Elena have?	What did she do?
She couldn't find her homeroom.	*The counselor took her there.*
She couldn't find her next class.	
She was nervous because she didn't speak English well.	
She couldn't find the cafeteria.	

b. Pairwork. Compare answers with your partner.

2. Ask volunteers to identify a problem that Elena had on her first day of school. Have them show where in the story they found the information. Let students read the story on their own to look for other problems Elena had.

Activity 5: List

1. *Part a.* Write this question on the board: *Where did Elena go on her first day at school?* Have students look back at the reading to find the answers. Let volunteers list the places on the board in the correct order.

2. Ask students to copy the first sentence in Activity 5 on another piece of paper. Read the second sentence and have the class complete it together. Ask them to write this sentence on their paper. Then have students work on their own to complete the remaining sentences.

3. *Part b.* Put students in pairs to compare ideas. Then ask one pair to read their sentences aloud for the class to compare.

Activity 6: Answer Questions

1. *Parts a and b.* Together study the chart on page 129. Read the first problem and ask students to look back at the story to find out what Elena did. Point out that the word *so* sometimes indicates the solution to a problem. For example, *I couldn't find my homeroom so she took me there.* Read the second problem aloud and let students tell what Elena did.

2. Give pairs of students a copy of AM 7/2. Have them work together to complete the chart. Then let pairs get together to compare answers.

Activity 7: Write

1. *Part a.* Give each student a copy of AM 7/3 or have them copy the chart on page 130. As a pre-writing activity, students can complete this chart, listing three or more problems they had on the first day of school. Then have them explain what they did in response to each problem. Circulate and assist students during this activity.

2. *Part b.* Using the ideas in their chart, students can write about their first day at this school.

3. *Part c.* Put students in pairs to share their stories. Tell them to listen to their partner's story and take notes in the second chart on AM 7/3.

4. *Part d.* Put pairs of students together to form groups of four. Have students take turns using their notes to tell about their partner's first day at school.

7. Write

a. On your own. What problems did you have on your first day at this school? List your ideas in a chart like this.

What problems did you have?	What did you do?

b. On your own. Use the ideas in your chart to write about your first day at this school.

c. Pairwork. Read your story to your partner. Listen carefully to your partner's story. Take notes in a chart like this.

What problems did your partner have?	What did your partner do?

d. Get together with another pair. Tell them about your partner's first day at school.

8. Predict

Classwork. In the story on pages 132–134, a man wants to build an oven, but he has a problem. What do you think is the problem? Make a prediction.

Maybe _____

_____

_____

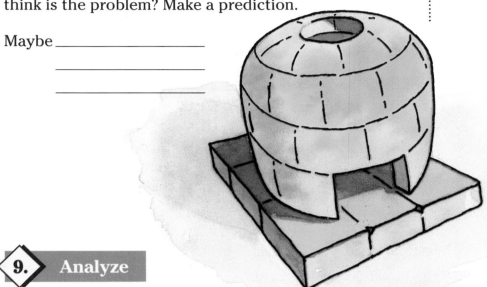

9. Analyze

a. Groupwork. Choose a picture on pages 132–134. Write several questions about the picture.

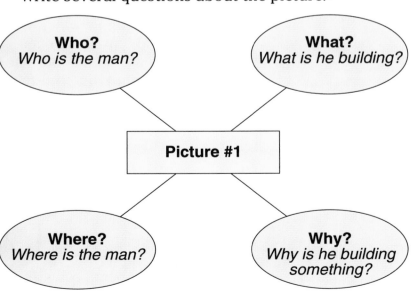

Who?
Who is the man?

What?
What is he building?

Picture #1

Where?
Where is the man?

Why?
Why is he building something?

b. Read your questions to the class. Let them guess answers to your questions.

Activity 8: Predict

1. Read the instruction line aloud and study the picture of the oven together. Explain that this type of oven is used to bake bread. Encourage students to look carefully at the oven and to ask questions. For example, *Why does it have a hole in the top? What is it made of?*

2. Read the instruction line again and let students predict answers to the question. List their ideas on the board, using the word *maybe*.

Activity 9: Analyze

1. *Part a.* Direct students to look at picture #1 on page 132 and ask them to describe what they see. Help them with unfamiliar vocabulary and write these words on the board. Repeat with the remaining pictures on pages 132–134.

2. Copy on the board the diagram in Activity 9 but delete the sample questions. Have students look again at picture #1 on page 132 and together think of questions beginning with *who, what, where,* or *why*. For example, *Who is the man?* Add their questions to the diagram on the board.

3. Have students get together in groups. Assign or have the groups choose one of the pictures on pages 132 –134. Tell them to study their picture and to write questions beginning with *who, what, where or why*. Circulate to help the groups with unfamiliar vocabulary.

4. *Part b.* Have each group share its questions while the rest of the class looks at the picture. Together predict answers to the questions.

Activity 10: Reader's Theater

1. Have students read the title of the story and guess which person in the pictures is Nasr-ed-Din.

2. Tell students that there are a narrator and four characters in this story. Have them look over the story to find the names of these people. Explain that Fatima is Nasr-ed-Din's wife, and Ali and Daoud are his friends.

3. Play the tape recorded version of the story or read it aloud. Together identify Nasr-ed-Din's problem. Play the tape again and let students read along.

4. Write this question on the board: *What does the word _____ mean?* Let students ask about any unfamiliar words in the story. Where possible, help them to use context clues to guess the meaning of a word.

10. Reader's Theater

Nasr-ed-Din's Oven

NARRATOR: Fatima and her husband, Nasr-ed-Din, lived in a small village. They didn't have an oven at home, so several times a week, Fatima baked her bread in the village oven.

FATIMA: I'm tired of going to the village oven to bake my bread. Some of my friends have ovens at home. Setare has a fine clay oven. Turan has an oven, too. And so does Ina.

NASR-ED-DIN: If you want an oven at home, I'll build one. I'll build it tomorrow.

NARRATOR: The next day, Nasr-ed-Din built an oven f Fatima. In the evening, his neighbor Ali came over to visit. Ali walked all around the new oven, shaking his head.

NASR-ED-DIN: What's wrong?

ALI: Your oven faces east.

NASR-ED-DIN: So what?

ALI: Don't you know which way the wind blows? An oven facing east is no good. The wind will put out your fire.

1

2

NARRATOR: The next morning, Nasr-ed-Din tore apart the oven. Then he built it again, facing west. He worked hard all day, and by evening, the oven was finished. He was admiring his new oven when his friend Daoud came over. Daoud walked all around the oven, shaking his head.

3

NASR-ED-DIN: What's wrong?

DAOUD: Your oven faces west.

NASR-ED-DIN: So what?

DAOUD: Don't you know which way the wind usually blows? An oven facing west is no good. There isn't enough air to start a fire.

4

5

NARRATOR: The next morning, Nasr-ed-Din tore apart his oven again. This time, he built the oven on an old cart with two wheels. He worked hard, and by evening, the oven was finished. Just then, Ali and Daoud came over to visit. They looked at the oven. They walked around it several times.

6

ALI: Why, oh why . . . ?

DAOUD: Why did you build your oven on top of a cart?

NASR-ED-DIN: I built it on a cart so that I can turn it in any direction—north, south, east, or west—whichever way my neighbors want it to face.

11. Share Ideas

Classwork. Share ideas about the story. Here are some questions you might think about.

1. Did you like the story? Why or why not?
2. How many times did Nasr-ed-Din build the oven?
3. How do you think Nasr-ed-Din felt at different times in the story? Why?
4. Do you think Nasr-ed-Din was a good problem solver? Why or why not?

12. Role Play

Groupwork. Get together in groups of five. Act out the story "Nasr-ed-Din's Oven."

13. Make a Plot Profile

a. Pairwork. What happened in the story? Add to the list of events below.

List of Events

1. Fatima asked Nasr-ed-Din to build an oven.
2. Nasr-ed-Din built an oven.
3. Ali came over.
4. Ali said the oven shouldn't face east.
5. Nasr-ed-Din tore apart the oven.
6. _____
7. _____
8. _____
9. _____
10. _____
11. _____
12. _____

Activity 11: Share Ideas

Discuss these questions as a class or have students work in groups to answer the questions. Then have groups report their answers to the class.

Activity 12: Role Play

Put students in groups of five to roleplay the story. Encourage students to use appropriate body language as they act out their role. Then let groups perform for the class.

Activity 13: Make a Plot Profile

1. *Part a.* Read aloud the instruction line and the five events in the list. Give pairs of students a copy of AM 7/4 and let them complete the list of events. Encourage students to look back at the story for information. (Possible answers: 6. Nasr-ed-Din built the oven facing west. 7. Daoud came over. 8. Daoud said the oven shouldn't face west. 9. Nasr-ed-Din tore apart the oven. 10. He built the oven on a cart. 11. Ali and Daoud came over. 12. Nasr-ed-Din said he built the oven to face any direction his neighbors wanted.) Compare answers as a class and agree on twelve events. List these events on the board to use in the next part of the activity.

(Continued on page 136.)

Activity 13: Make a Plot Profile (continued)

2. *Part b and c.* Have students study the plot profile on this page. Together find the horizontal and vertical axes and identify the information on each axis. Have students identify the first event in the story, using the list of events on the board. Together decide how interesting this event is on a scale from 1 to 10. Show students how to plot this information on the plot profile. Repeat with the second and third events in the story. Remind students that these are opinions, not facts.

3. Give pairs of students a copy of AM 7/5 or have them copy the plot profile. Give students time to plot the events in the story. Circulate to answer any questions. When students have charted the 12 events, have them connect the dots.

4. *Part d.* Have pairs compare plot profiles. Then post the plot profiles and have students look for similarities and differences. Based on the plot profiles, what were the most interesting events in the story?

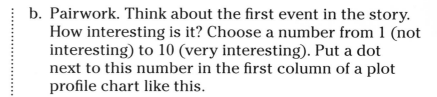

b. Pairwork. Think about the first event in the story. How interesting is it? Choose a number from 1 (not interesting) to 10 (very interesting). Put a dot next to this number in the first column of a plot profile chart like this.

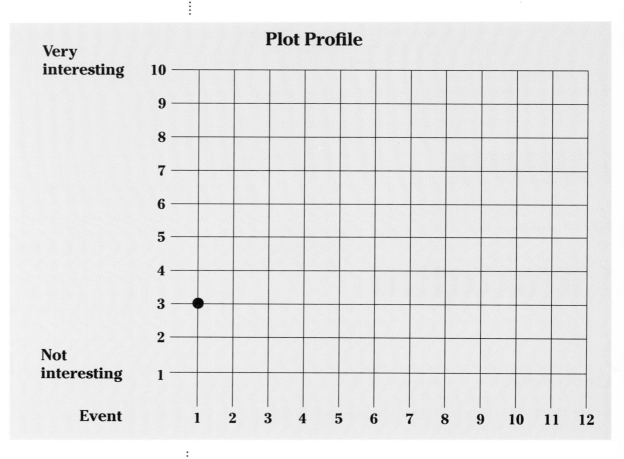

c. Repeat with the remaining events in the story. Then connect the dots.

d. Compare plot profiles with another pair.

14. Identify

a. Pairwork. What problems did Nasr-ed-Din have? How did he solve the problems? List your ideas in a chart like this.

Problem	Solution
Nasr-ed Din's wife wanted an oven at home.	→ Nasr-ed Din built an oven.

Problem	Solution
Nasr-ed Din's friend Ali said the oven shouldn't face east.	→

Problem	Solution
_____	→ _____

b. Compare charts with another pair.

15. Guess

Classwork. Study the pictures on pages 138–140. In each picture, someone has a problem. What do you think the problem is?

Picture #1: _____

_____

Picture #2: _____

_____

Picture #3: _____

_____

Language Focus

- Maybe the people don't like the man's ice cream.
- Maybe the man doesn't like to work outdoors.

Activity 14: Identify

1. *Part a.* Together identify the problems that Nasr-ed-Din had and list them on the board. Have students read the first example in the problem/solution chart on this page. Show students how to combine the problem and solution into one sentence, using *so.* (Nasr-ed-Din's wife wanted an oven at home, so he built one.)

2. Give pairs of students a copy of AM 7/6 or have them copy the chart on page 137. Have them work together to complete the chart.

3. *Part b.* Let pairs compare charts and then share their ideas with the class. Extend the activity by asking students to evaluate Nasr-ed-Din's solutions. Have them decide if they were excellent, very good, fair, or poor solutions to the problems.

Activity 15: Guess

1. Together study the pictures on pages 138-140. Have students describe what they see in each picture while you help with unfamiliar vocabulary. Introduce these words as you discuss the pictures: *ice cream stand, bowls, buttons, fasten, canvas.*

2. Tell students that someone in each of the pictures has a problem. Work together to suggest what the problems might be, using the models in the Language Focus box. List their ideas on the board.

Activity 16: Shared Reading

1. *Parts a and b.* Read the first problem aloud or play the tape. Together think of possible solutions to the problem, using the models in the Language Focus box. Let them write these on another piece of paper. Warn them not to write in the book.

2. Play the tape recorded version of Problems 2 and 3 or let students read them aloud in groups. Working in their groups, students can then come with possible solutions to the problems.

3. Let groups share their ideas with the class.

(Continued on page 141.)

16. Shared Reading

Language Focus

- Maybe he bought more bowls.
- Maybe he put the ice cream in cups.

a. Groupwork. Read about these three problems. For each problem, think of several possible solutions.

Problem 1	Possible Solutions
In 1904, Charles Menches sold bowls of ice cream from his outdoor ice cream stand. One very hot day, many people wanted to buy ice cream, but Menches didn't have enough bowls. What do you think he did? How did he solve his problem?	_____ _____ _____

Problem 2

A hundred years ago, many people wore shoes with buttons. It took a long time to fasten these shoes because they had a lot of buttons. Whitcomb Judson had a friend with a bad back. His friend couldn't button his shoes because his back hurt. Judson wanted to help his friend. What do you think he did?

Possible Solutions

_____

_____

_____

Problem 3

In 1848, a salesman traveled from New York to California. He took with him a large supply of canvas. Canvas is a very heavy material that people use to make tents. The salesman hoped to sell the canvas to gold prospectors—people who dig for gold. When he arrived in California, however, the prospectors didn't need tents. No one wanted to buy his canvas. What do you think he did?

Possible Solutions

_____

_____

_____

b. Read your lists of possible solutions to the class.

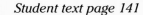

c. Compare your ideas with these solutions.

1. Next to Menches' ice cream stand, a man by the name of Ernest Hamwi was selling zalabia—a thin Persian waffle. Hamri rolled one of his waffles into a cone shape, and Menches put a scoop of ice cream into it. It was the first ice cream cone.

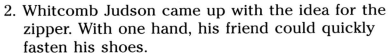

2. Whitcomb Judson came up with the idea for the zipper. With one hand, his friend could quickly fasten his shoes.

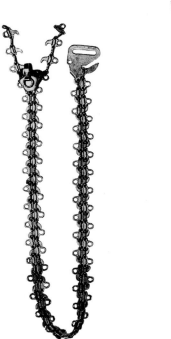

Activity 16: Shared Reading *(continued)*

Part c. Play the tape recorded versions of the solutions or have volunteers read them aloud. Encourage students to use context clues to guess the meaning of any unfamiliar words.

(Continued on page 142.)

Activity 17: Make a Chart

Part a. Give groups of students a copy of AM 7/7. Have them look back at pages 138-140 to find information to complete the chart. Circulate to answer any questions.

Part b. Put groups together to take turns asking and answering questions, using the information in their charts.

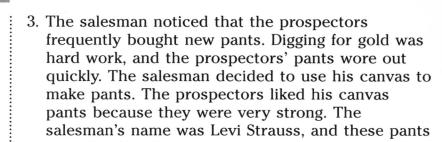

3. The salesman noticed that the prospectors frequently bought new pants. Digging for gold was hard work, and the prospectors' pants wore out quickly. The salesman decided to use his canvas to make pants. The prospectors liked his canvas pants because they were very strong. The salesman's name was Levi Strauss, and these pants were the first jeans.

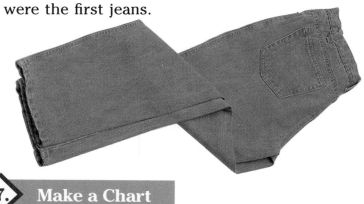

17. Make a Chart

a. Groupwork. Use the information on pages 138–142 to complete a chart like this.

Name	What problem did he have?	How did he solve the problem?
Charles Menches	*He didn't have the bowls to put his ice cream in.*	
Whitcomb Judson		
Levi Strauss		

b. Get together with another group. Take turns asking questions.

Q: What problem did _____ have?
A: _____ .
Q: How did he solve this problem?
A: _____ .

18. Design

a. Classwork. Read the information below.

During World War I (1914–1918), soldiers wore helmets like this:

After the war, the soldiers didn't need these helmets. To find new uses for the helmets, the magazine *Popular Mechanics* had a contest. It asked people to think of new ways to use the helmets. Here's one example:

b. Groupwork. What are some other ways to use these helmets? List your ideas.

You could use the helmets _____

_____ .

c. Groupwork. Choose one of your ideas. Draw a picture to illustrate it. Share your drawing with the class.

19. Guess

Classwork. What is the contraption or strange looking machine on the next page? What could you do with it? Share ideas with your classmates.

Activity 18: Design

Part a. Together read the information in Part a. Have students identify the problem (what to do with the helmets) and the solution in the book (use it to make a lamp).

Part b. Put students in groups to think of other ways to use the helmets. Have one member list the group's ideas.

Part c. Provide groups with newsprint and markers to illustrate one of their ideas. Display the pictures and have each group explain its idea.

Activity 19: Guess

Together study the picture on page 144. Have students suggest what you could do with this contraption, or strange machine.

Activity 20: Shared Reading

1. *Part a.* Have students read the title of this poem and suggest what the homework machine can do. Together think of things you would like to learn about this machine. For example, *How do you start it?* List these questions on the board and together think of possible answers.

2. Read the poem aloud. As you read, demonstrate the actions in the poem (put in your homework, drop in a dime, snap on the switch). Then let students read the poem aloud in different ways. For example, have the class read it together, have groups take turns reading a line, and/or let pairs read it to each other.

3. *Part b.* Have students take turns reading the poem aloud while their classmates show how to use the homework machine.

20. Shared Reading

a. Classwork. Listen to this poem. Then read it aloud with your classmates.

Homework Machine

The Homework Machine, oh, the Homework Machine,
Most perfect contraption that's ever been seen.
Just put in your homework, then drop in a dime,
Snap on the switch, and in ten seconds' time,
Your homework comes out, quick and clean as can be.
Here it is—"nine plus four?" and the answer is "three."
Three?
Oh me . . .
I guess it's not as perfect
As I thought it would be.

—*Shel Silverstein*

b. Classwork. Act out the poem.

21. Analyze

Pairwork. How does the homework machine work?
List the steps.

1. First, *put in your homework* .

2. Then, _____ .

3. Next, _____ .

4. In the end, *your homework comes out* .

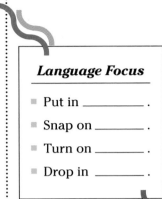

Language Focus

- Put in _____ .
- Snap on _____ .
- Turn on _____ .
- Drop in _____ .

22. Write

a. Groupwork. What kind of contraption would you like to have? Name it below.

The _____ Machine

b. Groupwork. What problem does your machine solve? Write a sentence telling what it does.

_____

_____

c. Groupwork. How does your contraption work? List the steps.

1. First, _____ .

2. Then, _____ .

3. Next, _____ .

4. Then, _____ .

5. In the end, _____ .

d. Groupwork. Use your ideas to write a poem. Then read your poem to the class.

Activity 21: Analyze

Together list the steps in using the homework machine, using the sentences in the Language Focus box. Then have students put the steps in the correct order by completing the sentences on page 145. Have them write their sentences on another piece of paper. (Answers: 1. First, put in your homework. 2. Then, drop in a dime. 3. Next, snap on the switch. 4. In the end, your homework comes out.)

Activity 22: Write

1. *Parts a, b, and c.* In this activity, students "invent" a problem-solving contraption and tell how it works. To get them started, work together to brainstorm some useful contraptions. For example, *The Answering Questions Machine, The Exercise Machine, The English Speaking Machine.* If students have trouble coming up with ideas, encourage them to think of problems they have or things that are difficult to do. They can then think of machines to solve these problems.

2. Put students in groups and give each group a copy of AM 7/8. Have the groups first choose a contraption and name it on their paper. Then have them write a sentence telling what the machine does. Finally, have them list the steps explaining how the machine works.

3. *Part d.* Students can use their ideas to write a poem about their contraption. Have them practice reading their poem aloud and encourage them to make changes until they like the way their poem sounds. Then have groups read their poem aloud to the class. Some students might want to illustrate the contraptions and display them in the classroom.

Activity Menu

Read the activities to the class and answer any questions. Then have students individually or in small groups select a project for a class or home-work assignment. Projects can be shared with the class and/or displayed in the classroom.

Activity Menu

Choose one of the following activities to do.

1. How Does It Work?
Bring to class a tool, kitchen gadget, or other piece of equipment. Teach your classmates how to use it. Together, think of other things you could use it for.

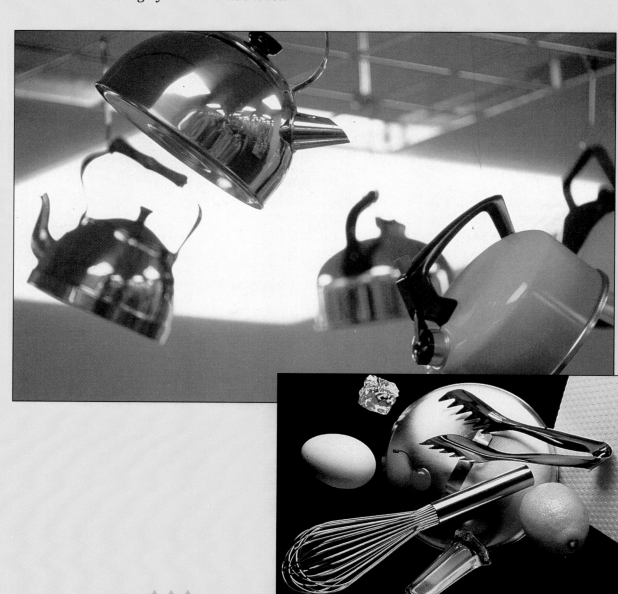

2. List the Steps

Watch someone use one of these machines:

- a copy machine
- a pay phone
- a fax machine
- a video recorder

List the steps for using the machine. Then act out the steps for your classmates.

3. Tell a Story

Write or retell a story. Read it to your classmates. Then ask them to make a plot profile of the story.

4. What's Your Advice?

List some of the problems newcomers to the United States might have. For each problem, tell what you could do to solve the problem. Put your ideas together in a booklet for newcomers. Give a copy of the booklet to your school counselor.

5. Find Out about an Invention

Look up the word *inventions* in the card catalog in a library. How many books about inventions are there? Choose one of the books and read about one invention. Tell the class what problem this invention solves. What does it help you to do?

Exploring Diversity

◇ 1. List

Classwork. *Diversity* means "variety." How many examples of diversity can you find in these pictures? List your ideas.

Examples of diversity:
- *many different languages*
- *many different kinds of clothing*
- _____

Activity 1: List

Read aloud the instruction line and the examples of diversity. Then have students study the pictures on pages 148 and 149 and identify other examples of diversity. List their ideas on the board.

Activity 2: Interview

1. *Parts a and b.* Tell students that they will interview a partner to see how they are alike and different. Let students dictate the questions in the chart on page 150 while you write them on the board. Then work with a student partner to model the activity. Write your answers to the questions in the first column of the chart. Ask your partner the questions and write the answers in the second column. Leave this chart on the board to use later.

2. Give each student a copy of AM 8/1 and have them write their own answers in the chart.

3. Put students in pairs to interview each other. Instruct them to write their partner's answers in their chart.

4. *Part c.* Copy on the board the Venn Diagram on page 150 but delete the examples. Write your name under the left circle. Write your partner's name under the right circle. Use your chart from Part a to complete the diagram. In the center area, list the ways you and your partner are similar. In the left circle list the ways you are different. In the right circle, list the ways your partner is different. Leave your completed Venn Diagram on the board to use later.

5. Have pairs draw and complete a Venn Diagram, using the information in their charts.

(Continued on page 151.)

2. Interview

Classwork. How are you and you classmates alike? How are you diverse, or different? Follow the instructions below to collect ideas.

a. On your own. Answer the questions in a chart like this.

	My Answers	My Partner's Answers
What languages do you speak?	English, Spanish	
Where were you born?	San Juan, Puerto Rico	
What is your favorite school subject?		
What is your favorite free time activity?		
Why are you studying English?		

b. Pairwork. Interview your partner. Add your partner's answers to the chart.
c. Pairwork. Which of your answers are the same? Which of your answers are different? Group your answers on a Venn Diagram.

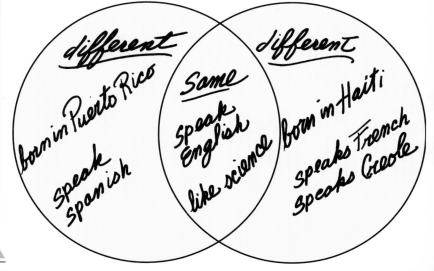

d. Pairwork. Share the information on your Venn Diagram with your classmates.

e. Classwork. Make a class chart on the board. Add information about each person in your class.

Language Focus

Similarities
- We both speak English.
- We both like science best.

Differences
- I speak Spanish and my partner speaks French and Creole.
- I was born in Puerto Rico, but my partner was born in Haiti.

Language	Birthplace	Favorite School Subject	Favorite Free Time Activity	Reasons for Studying English
English French	Puerto Rico			

f. Classwork. Count the number of different answers in each category.

g. Classwork. In which category is there the most diversity? In which category is there the least diversity?

Activity 2: Interview *(continued)*

6. *Part d.* Tell the class about the information in your Venn Diagram, using the models in the Language Focus box. For example, *We both speak English. I was born in the United States, but my partner was born in El Salvador.* Let your partner report information too.

7. Have pairs share the information in their Venn Diagram with the class.

8. *Part e.* Ask volunteers to copy on the board the chart on page 151. Then let students tell about their partner while a volunteer records the information in the chart. For example, *Sonia speaks English and Spanish.*

9. *Part f.* Have students total the number of **different** answers in each category and compare results. When they have agreed on a total, write it on the board.

10. *Part g.* Read the questions aloud and let students answer.

Activity 3: Compute

1. Read the title of the article aloud and ask students what it means to them. Together read the headings on the chart and look over the information. Ask what the first number in the chart refers to. (the number of people in the United States over the age of 5 who speak Spanish at home)

2. With less proficient students, practice reading the numbers aloud: *Seventeen million, three hundred thirty-nine thousand,* etc.

3. Write these questions on the board: *How many people over the age of five are there in the United States? How many of these people speak a language other than English?* Read the questions aloud and have students use context clues to guess the meaning of the words *over* and *other than* in the questions. Tell students to listen for answers to these questions as you read the passage. Then read the paragraph aloud to the class. Have students compare answers to the questions and show where in the paragraph they found the information.

(Continued on page 153.)

---

3. **Compute**

Pairwork. Read this information about language diversity in the United States and answer the questions on page 153.

Language Diversity in the United States

Today there are about 230,000,000 people in the United States over the age of five. About fourteen percent of these people speak a language other than English at home. What languages do these people speak? Look at the chart below to find out.

Language Used at Home	Total Speakers Over Five Years Old
Spanish	17,339,000
French	1,703,000
German	1,547,000
Italian	1,309,000
Chinese	1,249,000
Tagalog	843,000
Polish	723,000
Korean	626,000
Vietnamese	507,000
Portuguese	430,000
Japanese	428,000
Greek	388,000
Arabic	355,000
Hindu, Urdu, and related	331,000
Russian	242,000
Yiddish	213,000
Thai	206,000
Persian	202,000
French Creole	188,000
Armenian	150,000
Navaho	149,000
Hungarian	148,000
Hebrew	144,000
Dutch	143,000
Mon-Khmer	127,000

Questions

a. Fourteen percent of the people in the United States over the age of five speak a language other than English at home. How many people is that?

b. On a piece of paper, write your answer to the question in part "a."

Seventy-five percent of these people say they speak English "well" or "very well." How many people is that?

c. Is your first language listed in the chart? How many people in the United States speak your language?

d. Compare answers with your classmates.

 Preview

Classwork. Read the title of the story on the next page and study the pictures. What do you think the characters in the story are saying? Share ideas with your classmates.

To answer the question in part "a," follow these steps:

1. Reread the paragraph on page 152. Find the number of people in the United States over the age of five.

2. Multiply this number by fourteen percent (.14).

---

4. Read aloud the first question on page 153. Have students follow the steps in the box to find the answer. (Answer: 32,200,000.)

5. Have students write the answer to the first question (32,200,000) on a piece of paper. Then read the second question aloud. Students can work on their own or in pairs to answer the question. Then have students compare answers. (Answer: 24,150,000.) Have volunteers go to the board to explain how they arrived at the answer.

6. Read the third question aloud and give students time to look for their language in the chart on page 152. Students can then take turns reporting information from the chart. For example, *My first language is Tagalog. In the United States, 843,000 people over the age of 5 speak this language at home.*

Activity 4: Preview

1. Together read the title of the story on page 154. Have students identify the two languages in which the title is written. Ask speakers of other languages to translate the title into their own language and share it with the class. Write the words *mouse* and *mice* on the board. Point out that some words like *mouse* have an irregular plural form. Another example from the story is *child/children*.

2. Ask students to describe what they see in each picture. Encourage them to ask questions about the pictures and predict answers. For example, *Where are the mice? What are they doing?*

3. Ask students to guess what the characters in the story are saying. You can write their ideas on the board or give pairs of students a copy of AM 8/2 and have them write their ideas in the dialogue boxes. Keep their ideas to use later.

Activity 5: Shared Reading

1. Read the story aloud, using body language to illustrate the actions of the characters in the story. Read the story again or play the tape-recorded version.

2. Write this question on the board: *What does the word _____ mean?* Encourage students to ask about unfamiliar words in the story. Where possible, have them use context clues to guess the meaning of unfamiliar words.

3. Put students in groups of six to read and act out the story. Assign one student in each group to be the narrator while the remaining students choose story characters to roleplay. Then let the groups act out the story.

4. Animal sounds are expressed differently in different languages. Find out how your students express the sounds of a dog and a cat. Together make a chart on the board, identifying the languages and the animal sounds.

5. Shared Reading

Los Ratoncitos
(The Little Mice)

Once upon a time, a mother mouse and her young children went for a walk in the garden. They were looking around for something to eat when they suddenly heard a loud noise. "Hiss, Hiss, Meow!" It was *el gato,* the cat.

The mother mouse told her children to run and hide. The cat ran toward the mother mouse, but she didn't move. Instead, she stood up tall and looked him in the eye. She shook her fist at him. Then she yelled, "Woof, Woof, Woof!"

The cat heard the barking of a dog and was frightened. As quick as a wink, he ran away. The mother mouse called to her children and said, "You see, it's very important to know a second language."

6. Share Ideas

Classwork. What is your reaction to the story? Discuss your ideas with your classmates. Here are some questions to think about.

a. Did you like the story? Why or why not?
b. Look again at the pictures. What do you think the mouse is saying? Write your ideas.
c. A bilingual person can speak two languages. What are the advantages of being bilingual?
d. Being bilingual is helpful in many jobs. Can you think of some examples?

Activity 6: Share Ideas

1. *Parts a and b.* Give students a chance to talk freely about the story. Encourage them to tell what they liked or disliked about the story.

2. Together look back at AM 8/2 or at your list of ideas on the board from Activity 4. Have them add new ideas to the dialogue boxes based on the information in the story.

3. *Part c.* Read the instruction line aloud and together make a list of the advantages of being bilingual. For example, *A bilingual person can communicate with more people.*

4. *Part d.* Read the instruction line aloud and together think of some jobs in which being bilingual is helpful. Encourage students to tell why being bilingual is helpful in these jobs.

Activity 7: Make a Story Map

1. *Parts a and b.* Look over the story map together. Use the questions in the boxes to introduce these literary terms: *main characters, setting, problem, plot.*

2. Give each student a copy of AM 8/3. Let them work on their own to answer the questions in the story map. Circulate to support less proficient students. Make sure students do not write in the book.

3. Put students in pairs to compare story maps. If they disagree on an answer, encourage them to look back at the story to check their ideas. Next, let pairs get together in groups of four to compare answers. When the members of each group have agreed on answers, let the groups compare answers.

4. *Part c.* Model this part of the activity, working with a student partner. Use your story map to retell the beginning of the story. For example, you might start out by saying: *The title of this story is The Little Mice.* Then let your partner tell something about the story. For example, *This story is about a mother mouse and her three children.*

5. Put students in pairs to retell the story. Encourage them to take turns adding a line to the story. Let them use the story maps for ideas, but discourage them from looking back at the story.

7. Make a Story Map

a. On your own. Answer the questions in a story map like this.

Title: *Los Ratoncitos (The Little Mice)*

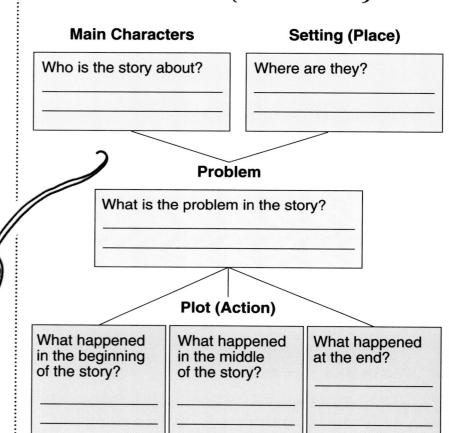

Main Characters

Who is the story about?
_____
_____

Setting (Place)

Where are they?
_____
_____

Problem

What is the problem in the story?
_____
_____

Plot (Action)

What happened in the beginning of the story? ____ ____	What happened in the middle of the story? ____ ____	What happened at the end? ____ ____

b. Compare story maps with your classmates.

c. Pairwork. Use your story map to retell the story *Los Ratoncitos.* Take turns adding a line to the story.

8. Write

a. Groupwork. Make up your own story about the importance of learning a second language. Choose animals or people as the characters in your story. Write your ideas in a story map.

Title: _____

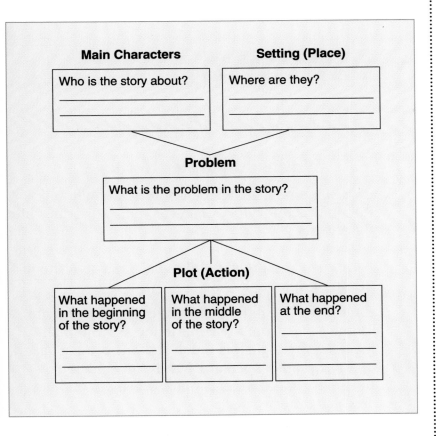

Main Characters

Who is the story about?
_____
_____

Setting (Place)

Where are they?
_____
_____

Problem

What is the problem in the story?
_____
_____

Plot (Action)

What happened in the beginning of the story?	What happened in the middle of the story?	What happened at the end?
_____ _____	_____ _____	_____ _____

b. Write or act out your story for your classmates.

Activity 8: Write

1. *Part a.* Tell students that they will write a story that teaches the same lesson as *Los Ratoncitos,* namely, that learning a second language is important. To further clarify the assignment, together choose an animal to serve as the main character in a story. Then together think of problems this animal might have. For example, you might choose a horse as the main character and some possible problems might be, *can't find food, is threatened by a wolf, can't find a warm place to sleep.* Then have students think of ways that being bilingual could help this animal solve her problems.

2. Put students in groups and give each group another copy of AM 8/3. Remind them that people or animals can be characters in their story. Encourage them to first list possible story ideas and then to choose the ideas they like best. When the members of a group have agreed on a story, have them add the information to their story map. It might take some groups a little time to get started, but encourage them to persist.

3. Circulate among the groups to answer any question and to help with unfamiliar vocabulary.

4. *Part b.* If you choose to have groups act out their stories, suggest that they choose a narrator to tell the story while other group members take the roles of different characters in their story.

5. If you choose to have them write their stories, provide them with newsprint. Have them write and illustrate their stories. Stories can later be read aloud and then displayed in the classroom.

Activity 9: Share Ideas

1. *Part a.* Write the terms *American culture* or *Canadian culture* on the board. Below this, list the words that come to mind when you think about this term. You might, for example, list ideas related to language, food, clothing, art, music, holidays, and customs. Try to include specific ideas, for example, *the Fourth of July, the Star Spangled Banner, family picnics, Oh, Canada, Confederation Day.* Encourage students to add other ideas that they associate with American or Canadian culture. If you have several students from the same cultural background, have them list the ideas that come to mind when they think of their culture.

2. Put students in groups of four to discuss the questions on page 158. Give the students in each group a number from 1 to 4. Tell them that each student in their group should be able to report their answers to the questions.

3. Call on the number 3s in each group to report their group's answer to the first question. Call on the number 1s to report their group's answer to the second question. Discuss any differences of opinion.

Activity 10: Use Context

1. Ask students to read the title of the article and the introduction. Then ask them to tell you about the person in the photograph.

2. Explain that this is an interview. One person, the interviewer, asks questions and Sandra Cisneros answers. Have students close their books for a minute and think of the questions they would like to ask Cisneros. Write their ideas on the board. Then have them scan the reading to find the questions that the interviewer asks. See if any of your questions are the same.

(Continued on page 159.)

a. **Groupwork.** Discuss these questions with your classmates.

- What do you think the word *bicultural* means?
- Many people are bilingual. Do you think it is also possible to be bicultural? Why or why not?

b. Report your group's ideas to the class.

Sandra Cisneros

Writing About Her Heritage

Sandra Cisneros is a Mexican-American poet and writer. In this interview, Cisneros talks about her life and her work.

INTERVIEWER: You grew up bilingual. Do you write in English or Spanish?

CISNEROS: I write in English. But everything I write about comes from my experience as a Spanish-speaker. My English is much richer because I grew up in a Spanish-speaking family. I feel lucky because I have twice as many words to choose from as other writers.

INTERVIEWER: What are your feelings about your Mexican-American heritage?

CISNEROS: My father is from Mexico City, so we visited Mexico a lot when I was growing up. It has always felt like a second home to me. In some ways, I feel more Mexican than American! I get very emotional when I cross the Mexican border or hear the Mexican national anthem.

INTERVIEWER: What would you like your readers to learn from your books?

CISNEROS: People's cultures are what make them special. People should never let go of their roots. My Mexican-American heritage is what made me the writer that I am today. I feel rich because I have two cultures inside of me.

11. Use Context

a. Classwork. Choose a word to complete these sentences. More than one word may be possible.

1. My English is much richer because I grew up in a Spanish-speaking family. I feel _____ because I have twice as many words to choose from as other writers.

   sad   happy   cold   tired   smart

   Find the word *lucky* on page 158. What do you think this word means?

2. Mexico has always felt like a second home to me. In some ways I feel more Mexican than American! I get very _____ when I cross the Mexican border, or hear the Mexican national anthem.

   hungry   happy   sad   excited

   Find the word *emotional* on page 158. What do you think this word means?

3. People's cultures are what make them special. People should never let go of their _____. My Mexican-American heritage is what made me the writer that I am today.

   problems   culture   heritage   money   family

   Find the word *roots* at the top of this page. What do you think this word means?

Activity 10: Use Context (continued)

3. Choose one student to read the interviewer's questions while you read Cisneros' answers. Then give students time to read the interview silently.

4. Encourage students to point out anything that interested or surprised them in the interview.

Activity 11: Use Context

1. Explain to students that they will often come across new words when they read. Sometimes they will be able to figure out the meaning of a new word by using context, or the words and ideas around the new word.

2. Read the first sentence aloud and have students choose the word or words that could complete this sentence. Then have them find the sentence with the word *lucky* on page 158. Let a student read this sentence aloud and then have students use context to guess the meaning of the word *lucky*. Note that the goal is to come up with an approximate definition of the word.

3. Repeat with the remaining sentences.

Activity 12: Take Notes in a Chart

1. *Part a.* Put students in groups and give each group a copy of AM 8/4 or have them copy the chart on page 160. Have volunteers take turns reading the questions in the chart aloud. Answer any questions about unfamiliar words.

2. Have students work in their groups to write answers to the questions in the chart. Encourage them to look back at the reading for information.

3. *Part b.* Pair up the groups and have them take turns asking and answering the questions in the chart. Go over the answers as a class and discuss any differences of opinion.

Activity 13: Evaluate

1. *Part a.* Put students in groups of four to discuss the two statements. Give the students in each group a number from 1 to 4. Remind them that each student in a group should be able to report their group's answers.

2. *Part b.* Call out a number from 1 to 4 and have those students report their group's response to the first statement. Repeat for the second statement.

12. Take Notes in a Chart

a. Groupwork. What do you know about Sandra Cisneros? Look back at the reading and take notes in a chart like this.

Sandra Cisneros

What is her occupation?	
What languages does she speak?	
How does she feel about being bilingual?	
How does she feel about her heritage (roots)?	
Why does she think roots are important?	

b. Ask your classmates the questions in the chart. Compare answers.

13. Evaluate

a. Groupwork. Do you agree with these ideas? Why or why not?

- People's cultures are what make them special.
- People should never let go of their roots.

b. Report your group's ideas to the class. Tell why you agree or disagree.

14. Study a Picture

a. On your own. This painting gives information about one person's roots. Study the picture for one minute.

Carmen Lomas Garza is a Mexican-American painter. This painting is based on memories of her childhood in Texas.

Activity 14: Study a Picture

1. *Part a.* Together read the information about the painter at the bottom of the page. Tell students that you will give them one minute to study the picture. Encourage them to look carefully at the different parts of the painting. Then time one minute. When the minute is up, ask students to close their books.

(Continued on page 162.)

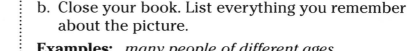

Activity 14: Study a Picture *(continued)*

2. *Part b.* Tell students to think about the picture and to list everything they remember. Read the examples to help them get started. Then give them time to write their ideas.

3. *Part c.* Put students in groups to compare lists. Then have them combine the ideas on their lists to make one group list. Each group can then write its list on the board. Together compare the lists on the board. Look back at the painting to check the lists for accuracy.

4. *Part d.* Review Wh-questions, using the sample questions in the Language Focus box. Have students look back at the painting and suggest answers to these questions.

5. *Part e.* Put students in pairs to write several questions about the painting. Circulate to provide support.

6. Have pairs take turns reading their questions to the class. Encourage one person in each pair to point to the appropriate place in the picture while the other person reads the question aloud. Let the class think of possible answers to the questions.

7. *Part f.* Give students time to write about Garza's childhood memory. Some students might find it easier to write from the painter's point of view or from the point of view of someone in the painting, using the first person. They might want to imagine that they are describing this event in a letter to a friend. Encourage students to start with some general information about the event: *Where it took place, when it took place, who was there?* They can then move on to a more detailed description.

8. Let students choose a way to share their writing with their classmates. For example, they could read their writing to a partner or group of classmates, post their writing on a classroom wall, or make a class booklet of writing.

9. *Part g.* Give students time to think about the questions, and then have them share ideas with their classmates.

b. Close your book. List everything you remember about the picture.

Examples: *many people of different ages*
they are outdoors
a dog
two boys are playing marbles

c. Compare lists with your classmates.

d. Pairwork. Look at the picture again. Write several questions about the picture.

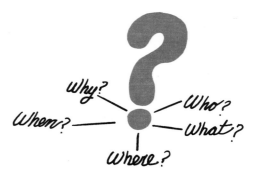

e. Pairwork. Read your questions to the class. (You can point to people in the picture.) Together, think of possible answers.

f. On your own. Carmen Lomas Garza painted a picture of a childhood memory. How would you describe her memory in words? Write your description on another piece of paper.

g. Classwork. What does this painting tell you about Carmen Lomas Garza's roots? What do you know about her? Share ideas with your classmates.

Language Focus

■ Who is the girl in the middle?

■ What are the two boys in the corner doing?

■ Where are these people?

■ Why is the girl hitting the fish?

---

15. Make a Cluster Diagram

a. On your own. What do you remember about your childhood? Follow the steps below to collect your ideas on a cluster diagram.

1. Think about your childhood. Write anything you think of on a cluster diagram.

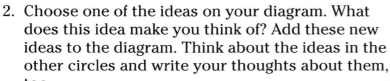

2. Choose one of the ideas on your diagram. What does this idea make you think of? Add these new ideas to the diagram. Think about the ideas in the other circles and write your thoughts about them, too.

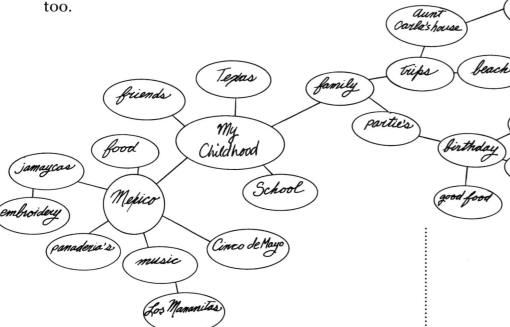

Activity 15: Make a Cluster Diagram

1. Introduce this activity by making a cluster diagram on the board with information about your childhood. You can also use the model on page 163, but it is more useful for students to watch someone go through the actual process of making a cluster diagram. Start by writing the words *my childhood* on the board and circling them. Think about this topic and write down the words that come to mind. Don't pick and choose, just write the words down. Circle each word as you write it and then draw a line connecting it to the most closely related word on your diagram.

2. Have students work on their own to make a cluster diagram about their childhood. Encourage them to write down words in their first language if they don't know a word in English. They can go back later and translate the word with help from you or a classmate.

Activity 16: Think–Pair–Share

1. *Part a.* Model this activity by telling students about one of the ideas on your cluster diagram. Then have students choose one of the ideas on their cluster diagram. Give them a few minutes to think about this childhood memory.

2. Put students in pairs to share stories. Remind them to listen carefully to their partner's story. Later they will retell their partner's story.

3. *Part b.* Encourage students to ask each other questions to make sure they understood their partner's story.

4. *Part c.* Have pairs get together in groups of four. Give them time to retell their partners' stories.

16. Think-Pair-Share

a. Pairwork. Choose one of the memories on your cluster diagram. Tell your partner about this special memory. Listen carefully to your partner's story.

b. Ask each other questions about your memories.

c. Get together with another pair.
Tell your partner's story.

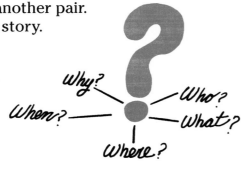

Activity Menu

Read the activities to the class and answer any questions. Then have students individually or in small groups select a project for a class or homework assignment. Projects can be shared with the class and/or displayed in the classroom.

Activity Menu

Choose one of the following activities to do.

1. Make a Collage
Look in magazines for pictures with examples of diversity. Use the pictures to make a collage. Show your collage to your classmates and have them find the examples of diversity.

2. Interview Your Classmates
Interview the people in your class to learn about your similarities and differences. First, prepare a list of questions to ask your classmates. Then collect your classmates' answers. Show the results of your interviews on a chart.

3. Explore Language Diversity at Your School
What languages do the students at your school speak at home? Prepare a questionnaire to collect information. Then give the questionnaire to the students of another class.

4. Interview a Bilingual Person
Interview a bilingual person—someone outside of class. Find out how this person uses two languages. Tell the class what you learned.

5. Read a Story
Look in a library for the book *The House on Mango Street* by Sandra Cisneros. Read one of the stories in the book and tell your classmates about it.

6. Draw a Picture
Draw a picture of a childhood memory. Show your picture to the class and answer their questions.

7. Collect Words in Different Languages
Choose a word in your first language. Translate this word into any other languages you know. Talk to people who speak other languages. Learn how to say this word in their language. Then find or draw a picture to illustrate this word. Around the picture, list the different ways to say this word.

8. Share Stories
Bring in something from home that gives information about you and your heritage. This might be a photograph, an article of clothing, some food, some music, or a game. Show it to your classmates and answer their questions.

TAPESCRIPT BOOK 1

Unit One: Getting Around School

Activity 1. Listen and find the person.

This is Fernando. He is from Mexico.
This is Marta. She is from Russia.
This is Satoshi. He's from Japan.
This is Ali. He's from Iran.
This is Claudia. She's from Colombia.
This is Nadine. She's from Haiti.

Unit Two: Spending Free Time

Activity 2. Listen and find the person.

I like to listen to music in my free time.
I like to talk on the telephone.
I like to play soccer.
I like to watch TV in my free time.
I like to go shopping.
I like to play volleyball in my free time.
I like to play the guitar.

Activity 5. Listen and record each person's answer.

A: Do you like to listen to music?
B: Yes, I do.

A: Do you like to talk on the telephone?
B: No, I don't.

A: Do you like to play soccer?
B: Yes, I do. I love soccer.

A: Do you like to go shopping?
B: No, I don't.

A: Really?
B: Really.

A: Do you like to watch TV?
B: Yes, I do.

Activity 8. Listen and find the person.

Do you want to play basketball?
Sure. I'd love to.

Let's play soccer.
Great idea.

Let's go shopping.
Sorry, I can't.

Do you want to go to the beach?
I'd love to, but I'm busy.

Activity 9. Listen and compare ideas.

I'd Love To

I'd love to play basketball, but I don't have a hoop.
I'd love to write a letter, but I don't have a pen.
I'd love to go fishing, but I don't have a pole.
I'd love to paint a picture, but I don't have a brush.
I'd love to go surfing, but I don't have a board.
I'd love to play volleyball, but I don't have a net.
But I do have a guitar, so let's play some music.

Activity 10. Listen and read along.

Chess is popular at Junior High School 43 in Harlem, New York. Every day at lunch time students get together to play chess. After school, some of the students play three or four more hours.

Stephen Barton, a high school student in Hernando Beach, Florida, likes to build things—big things. He spent hundreds of hours at the computer and in the library, learning about submarines. Then he built this submarine in his basement.

Activity 14, part b. Listen and check your answers.

Nina gets up at six o'clock in the morning.
She leaves home at 7:30.
She gets to school at 8 o'clock.
School ends at 2:30.
After school, she has some free time.
At 6:30, she has dinner.
After dinner, she does her homework.
At ten o'clock in the evening, she goes to bed.
She has some free time in the afternoon between 3 and 5.
She has some free time in the evening between 8 and 10.

Activity 16. Listen to the chant.

Hey man, I'm feeling blue.
There's nothing at all for me to do.

Play ball, read a book.
What do you mean there's nothing to do?

Unit Three: Counting Dollars and Cents

Activity 1. Listen and find the amount of money.

twenty-five cents
one cent
ten cents
five cents

a nickle
a quarter
a dime
a penny

one dollar
twenty dollars
five dollars
ten dollars

Activity 3, part a. Listen and point to the number.

zero
one
two
three
four
five
six
seven
eight
nine
ten
eleven
twelve
thirteen
fourteen
fifteen
sixteen
seventeen
eighteen
nineteen
twenty
twenty-one
twenty-two
thirty
forty
fifty
sixty
seventy
eighty
ninety
one hundred
one thousand

Now find these numbers.

ten	eighteen
six	thirteen
nine	eleven
five	fifteen
eight	seventeen
four	twelve
	twenty
	fourteen
	nineteen
	sixteen

fifty
ninety
forty
twenty-two
sixty
seventy
thirty
eighty

one thousand
one hundred

Activity 3, part b. Listen and circle the number.

thirty . . . thirty
fourteen . . . fourteen
fifteen . . . fifteen
sixteen . . . sixteen
seventy . . . seventy
eighty . . . eighty
nineteen . . . nineteen

Activity 5. Listen and write the price.

A: Excuse me. How much does this dictionary cost?
B: Twelve dollars and ninety-five cents.
A: Thanks.

A: Excuse me. How much does this walkman cost?
B: Twenty-five dollars.
A: Thanks.

A: Excuse me. How much does this watch cost?
B: Thirty-five dollars.
A: Thanks.

A: How much does this backpack cost?
B: Seventeen dollars and fifty cents.
A: Thanks.

A: How much does this pen cost?
B: Fifty-five cents.
A: Thanks.

A: How much does this calculator cost?
B: Nine dollars and ninety-five cents.
A: Thanks.

Listen and check your answers.

Activity 10. Listen and write the total amount of each order.

A: I'd like a hamburger and a small soda, please.
B: That will be three dollars and sixty-four cents.

A: I'd like a taco and a small glass of milk, please.
B: That will be two dollars and twenty-nine cents.

A: I'd like a salad, a hot dog, and a small soda, please.
B: That will be five dollars and thirty-four cents.

A: I'd like a peanut butter sandwich and a glass of water, please.
B: That will be one dollar and seventy-five cents.

Listen and check your answers.

Unit Four: Choosing Clothes

Activity 1. Listen and identify the clothes.

gym shorts
skirt
sweatshirt
dress
boots
jacket
coat
woman's suit
man's suit
baseball cap
socks
blue jeans
sweater
athletic shoes
shirt and tie
sweatpants
T-shirt

Activity 3, pages 64 and 65. Listen and study the picture on page 64.

This is a picture of me and my friends. My friend Martin is wearing a suit and tie. My friend Fernando is wearing blue sweatpants. Greg is the person wearing blue jeans and a T-shirt. He's my best friend. My friend Tony is wearing shorts and a T-shirt. What am I wearing?

Listen and check your answer.

Now listen and study the picture on page 65.

This is a picture of me and my friends. My friend Deborah is wearing a brown skirt. She's from Costa Rica. Anna is the person wearing blue sweatpants and a blue sweatshirt. She likes to play soccer. My friend Jane is wearing blue jeans and a red sweater. She likes to play chess. Maria is the person wearing blue jeans and a jacket. What am I wearing?

Listen and check your answer.

Activity 5, part b, page 67. Listen and write the price for each article of clothing.

A: Excuse me. How much does this red sweater cost?
B: Eighteen dollars.
A: Thanks.

A: Excuse me. How much does this sweatshirt cost?
B: Twelve dollars.
A: Thanks.

A: Excuse me. How much does this T-shirt cost?
B: Nine dollars.
A: Thanks.

A: Excuse me. How much do the plaid pants cost?
B: Twenty-four dollars.
A: Thanks.

A: Excuse me. How much do the brown pants cost?
B: Thirty-two dollars.
A: Thanks.

A: Excuse me, how much do these blue jeans cost?
B: Twenty-eight dollars.
A: Thanks.

A: Excuse me. How much do the brown shoes cost?
B: Twenty-five dollars.
A: Thanks.

A: Excuse me. How much do the white sneakers cost?
B: Forty-five dollars.
A: Thanks.

A: Excuse me. How much do the red shoes cost?
B: Eighteen dollars.
A: Thanks.

A: Excuse me. How much do the black shoes cost?
B: Thirty-six dollars.
A: Thanks.

Activity 13. Listen to this poem.

Ode to My Shoes

My shoes from America,
they are very expensive and soft.
They help me to walk.
When I go somewhere,
they go with me, too.
They come to school with me.
When I go back home,
my shoes stay under my bed.
Sometimes they look very happy.
When they are torn,
they look like they are smiling.
When they are dirty,
they look very sleepy.
I like my shoes.

Unit 5: Checking the Weather

Activity 1. Listen and point to the cities.

It's raining in Beijing.
It's cloudy in Rome.
It's hot in Cairo.
It's storming in Dallas.
It's snowing in Quebec City.
It's hot and sunny in San Juan.
It's cold in Juneau.
It's sunny and windy in Montreal.

Listen again.

Activity 2, pages 84 and 85. Listen and identify these cities.

It's sunny and warm in Mexico City.
It's sunny and cold in Chicago.
It's snowing in Portland.
It's cloudy in Vancouver.
It's raining in Boston.
It's windy in Toronto.

Activity 4. What are they going to do tomorrow? Listen and complete a chart.

Dialogue 1

A: What do you want to do tomorrow?
B: I don't know. I think it's going to rain.
A: Then let's go to a movie.
B: Okay.

Dialogue 2

A: What do you want to do tomorrow?
B: I don't know. I think it's going to be sunny.
A: Then let's do something outdoors.
B: Okay.

Listen and check your answers.

Activity 16. Listen to the story.

The North Wind and the Sun

NARRATOR: One day, the north wind and the sun got into an argument.

NORTH WIND: I'm stronger than you.

SUN: Impossible! I'm much stronger than you.

NORTH WIND: Never! I am stronger.

NARRATOR: Just then, the north wind saw a traveler walking on the road below.

NORTH WIND: Let's test our strength on that traveler. I'm sure I can make her take off her coat faster than you can.

SUN: Impossible. I'm certain to win.

NARRATOR: The north wind tried first. He blew down hard on the traveler. He blew harder and harder, but the traveler held onto her coat.

SUN: Now it's my turn.

NARRATOR: At first, the sun shone gently on the traveler, who soon unbuttoned her coat. Then the sun shone in full strength. Before long, the traveler took off her coat and continued her journey without it.

Unit 6: Making Journeys

Activity 6. Listen and read along.

Crossing Antarctica

Antarctica, the land of the South Pole, is the world's coldest, iciest, and windiest continent. Scientists have recorded a temperature of minus 128.6°F (−89.2°C) in Antarctica! Ice more than a mile thick covers 98 percent of the land. Along the coast, scientists have recorded winds of up to 200 miles (322 kilometers) an hour.

Almost no life can exist in the interior of Antarctica. Along its shores and in the surrounding waters, however, a variety of wildlife lives. Penguins, seals, whales, and many kinds of fish swim in the ocean surrounding Antarctica.

In 1989, a six-person team spent 221 days traveling across the continent of Antarctica. The team included scientists and explorers from the former Soviet Union, China, Japan, France, Britain, and the United States. They traveled across the continent on cross-country skis while 36 dogs pulled their equipment.

The team traveled an average of 17 miles a day. Sometimes, the traveling was difficult and dangerous. Strong winds and snow made it difficult to see and the explorers worried about getting lost. They also had to cross an area with crevasses in the ice. Many times, the dogs fell into these deep holes and the explorers had to pull them out.

"It's really like another planet," said one team member. "The weather is always trying to kill you. It's typically 30 degrees below zero with winds of 30 miles per hour. That's a common day."

Unit 7: Solving Problems

Activity 1.

These students moved to North America last year. What problems did they have when they arrived here? Listen and complete the sentences.

I couldn't understand my teachers.

I didn't know anyone at school.

People couldn't say my name.

I couldn't eat the food. It was very different from the food in my country.

I didn't speak English very well.

Sometimes I got homesick.

Listen and check your answers.

Activity 4. Listen to the story.

My First Day at School

My first day at this school was January 15, 1992. When I first got to school, I went to the office. The counselor in the office gave me a class schedule. I couldn't find my homeroom so she took me there. I was really happy in this class because all the students spoke Spanish. When homeroom finished, my new friends helped me to find my next class. When I got to this class, there were only two students, and they didn't speak Spanish. I was really nervous because I didn't speak English very well. I tried to relax and do my best, but it wasn't easy.

At noon, I had to go to the cafeteria, but I didn't know where it was. I didn't see any Spanish-speaking students in the hallway, so I asked a teacher. He told me that the cafeteria was on the first floor. After lunch, I had three more classes. Many students spoke Russian, and I couldn't understand them. I tried to speak English with them, and they seemed friendly. After school, I went home. This was my first day in school.

Activity 10. Listen to this story.

Nasr-ed-Din's Oven

NARRATOR: Fatima and her husband, Nasr-ed-Din, lived in a small village. They didn't have an oven at home, so several times a week, Fatima baked her bread in the village oven.

FATIMA: I'm tired of going to the village oven to bake my bread. Some of my friends have ovens at home. Setare has a fine clay oven. Turan has an oven too. And so does Ina.

NASR-ED-DIN: If you want an oven at home, I'll build one. I'll build it tomorrow.

NARRATOR: The next day, Nasr-ed-Din built an oven for Fatima. In the evening, his neighbor Ali came over to visit. Ali walked all around the new oven, shaking his head.

NASR-ED-DIN: What's wrong?

ALI: Your oven faces east.

NASR-ED-DIN: So what?

ALI: Don't you know which way the wind blows? An oven facing east is no good. The wind will put out your fire.

Narrator: The next morning, Nasr-ed-Din tore apart the oven. Then he built it again, facing west. He worked hard all day, and by evening, the oven was finished. He was admiring his new oven when his friend Daoud came over. Daoud walked all around the oven shaking his head.

NASR-ED-DIN: What's wrong?

DAOUD: Your oven faces west.

NASR-ED-DIN: So what?

DAOUD: Don't you know which way the wind usually blows? An oven facing west is no good. There isn't enough air to start a fire.

NARRATOR: The next morning, Nasr-ed-Din tore apart his oven again. This time, he built the oven on an old cart with two wheels. He worked hard, and by evening, the oven was finished. Just then, Ali and Daoud came over to visit. They looked at the oven. They walked around it several times.

ALI: Why, oh why . . . ?

DAOUD: Why did you build your oven on top of a cart?

NASR-ED-DIN: I built it on a cart so that I can turn it in any direction—north, south, east, or west—whichever way my neighbors want it to face.

Activity 16. Listen and read along.

Problem 1

In 1904, Charles Menches sold bowls of ice cream from his outdoor ice cream stand. One very hot day, many people wanted to buy ice cream, but Menches didn't have enough bowls. What do you think he did? How did he solve his problem?

Problem 2

A hundred years ago, many people wore shoes with buttons. It took a long time to fasten these shoes because they had a lot of buttons. Whitcomb Judson had a friend with a bad back. His friend couldn't button his shoes because his back hurt. Judson wanted to help his friend. What do you think he did?

Problem 3

In 1848, a salesman traveled from New York to California. He took with him a large supply of canvas. Canvas is a very heavy material that people use to make tents. The salesman hoped to sell the canvas to gold prospectors—people who dig for gold. When he arrived in California, however, the prospectors didn't need tents. No one wanted to buy his canvas. What do you think he did?

Compare your ideas with these solutions:

Problem 1. Next to Menches' ice cream stand, a man by the name of Ernest Hamwi was selling zalabia—a thin Persian waffle. Hamwi rolled one of his waffles into a cone shape, and Menches put a scoop of ice cream into it. It was the first ice cream cone.

Problem 2. Whitcomb Judson came up with the idea for the zipper. With one hand, his friend could quickly fasten his shoes.

Problem 3. The salesman noticed that the prospectors frequently bought new pants. Digging for gold was hard work, and the prospectors' pants wore out quickly. The salesman decided to use his canvas to make pants. The prospectors liked his canvas pants because they were very strong. The salesman's name was Levi Strauss, and these pants were the first jeans.

Unit 8: Exploring Diversity

Activity 5. Listen to this story.

Los Ratoncitos (The Little Mice)

Once upon a time, a mother mouse and her young children went for a walk in the garden. They were looking around for something to eat when they suddenly heard a loud noise. "Hiss, Hiss Meow!" It was *el gato,* the cat.

The mother mouse told her children to run and hide. The cat ran toward the mother mouse, but she didn't move. Instead, she stood up tall and looked him in the eye. She shook her fist at him. Then she yelled, "Woof, Woof, Woof!"

The cat heard the barking of a dog and was frightened. As quick as a wink, he ran away. The mother mouse called her children and said, "You see, it's very important to know a second language."

Text permissions

We wish to thank the authors, publishers, and holders of copyright for their permission to reprint the following:

Excerpts from *Sandra Cisneros: Writing About Her Heritage* from *U.S. Express*, February, 1991. Copyright © 1991 by Scholastic, Inc. Reprinted by permission of Random House.

The Harder They Come by James Chambers (Jimmy Cliff). Copyright © 1972 Reprinted by permission of Polygram Music Publishers, Inc.

Photo Credits

Unit 1

Chapter Opener
xx,1 © Richard Hutchings/Photo Researchers, Inc.

Text
3 Left to Right: © Susan Van Etten, © Shirley Zeiberg/Photo Reseachers, Inc.
4 Clockwise from top right: © Index Stock, © Rhoda Sidney/Monkmeyer Press, © Jeff Greenberg/The Picture Cube, © Steven Cohen/Index Stock
5 Clockwise from top left: © Index Stock, © Dennis McDonald/The Picture Cube, © Spencer Grant/The Picture Cube, © Stock Imagery
7 © Jeffrey Meyer/Stock Imagery
8 © Jeffrey Meyer/Stock Imagery
10 Clockwise from top left: © Robert Daemmrich/Tony Stone Worldwide Ltd.,© Larry Lawfer/The Picture Cube, © Robert Brenner/PhotoEdit, © Owen Franken/Stock Boston, © Brent Jones/Stock Boston
11 Clockwise from top right: © Stock Imagery, © Aneal Vohra/Unicorn Stock, © Stock Imagery, © Martin Jones/Unicorn Stock
12 Clockwise from bottom left: Stephen Frisch/Stock Boston, © Jim Zuckerman/Westlight, © Bob Daemmrich/The Image Works, © Spencer Grant/Monkmeyer Press
13 Clockwise from top left: © Jeffrey Meyers/Stock Imagery, © Jeff Greenberg/Unicorn Stock Photos, © Freeman/Grishaber/PhotoEdit
14 © Robert Brenner/PhotoEdit

Unit 2

Chapter Opener
16 Clockwise from top left: © Georgen Goodwin/Monkmeyer Press, © Michal Herron/Woodfin Camp and Assoc., © Comstock, Mimi Forsyth/Monkmeyer Press, © Rob Crandall/ Stock Boston, © Rick Kopstein/Monkmeyer Press
17 Clockwise from top left: Bob Daemmrich/Stock Boston, © Index Stock, © Jeff Greenberg/Photo Researchers, Inc., © R. Sydney/The Image Works

Text
18 Top to bottom: © Index Stock, © B. Daemmrich/The Image Works
19 Clockwise from top left: © Index Stock, © Index Stock, © The Picture Cube, © Sullivan/Index Stock
21 Clockwise from top left: © Richard Hutchings/Photo Researchers Inc., © Jeff Greenberg/Photo Researcher Inc., © Bob Daemmrich/Stock Boston, © Index Stock, © Peter Vandermark/Stock Boston
23 Clockwise from top left: © Arthur Tilley/FPG Int'l., Eric Kopstein/Monkmeyer Press, © Ellis Herwig/The Picture Cube, © Rhoda Sidney/The Image Works
25 © Index Stock
26 Clockwise from top left: © Mike and Carol Werner/Comstock, © Bruce Ando/Index Stock, © Stock Imagery, © Mike and Carol Werner, Comstock
28 Clockwise from top left: Edward Keating, Peter Britton, Peter Britton, Peter Britton
29 Left to right: © Comstock, © Comstock
31 © Comstock
35 © James Lemass/The Picture Cube

Unit 3

Chapter Opener
36 3PO

Text
51 © Comstock
54 Clockwise from top left: The Smithsonian Institution, Nation Museum of American History, National Numismatic Collection, © Stock Imagery, © Stock Imagery, © Stock Imagery, From the World Book Encyclopedia. © 1993 World Book Inc., By permission of the publisher, From the World Book Encyclopedia. © 1993 World Book Inc., By permission of the publisher